MARROW
Basil

MEAT
Garlic

MEAT PIES
Peppercorn

MUSTARD PICKLES
Turmeric

MUSTARD SAUCE
Mustard

MUTTON
Capers

PEAS
Basil

PICKLES
Tarragon

PIMMS
Borage

POTATO SALAD
Dill

ROAST BEEF
Horse-Radish

ROLLS
Poppy Seeds

SALADS
Chervil, Garlic, Hyssop, Nasturtium, Savory, Sorrel, Tarragon, Chives

SALAD DRESSING
Dill

SAUCES
Tarragon

SAUTE POTATOES
Rosemary

SAVOURIES
Sorrel

SAVOURY RICE
Cayenne Pepper, Saffron

SOUPS
Balm, Basil, Bay, Celery Seed, Dill, Marjoram, Rosemary, Savory, Hyssop, Pot Herbs, Thyme

SPAGHETTI BOLOGNAISE
Oregano

STUFFINGS
Chives, Lemon Thyme, Oregano, Sage, Thyme

TARTARE SAUCE
Capers

TOMATO
Basil, Paprika (Tomato Sauce), Thyme

VEAL
Mint

VEGETABLES
Mace, Parsley

JUNIPER

Small blue berries with a spicy pungent taste, used fresh or dried in marinade for game, more especially for venison.

MACE

Prepared from the covering of nutmeg seed. Blade mace flavours vinegars and Bechamel Sauce. Use ground mace in vegetables, cakes.

MUSTARD

A widely used condiment, the English variety being sold as a powder. Mustard sauce is delicious with mackerel, or with lambs tongues.

OREGANO

A type of marjoram, stronger, more pungent, used in stuffing, meat sauce for Spaghetti Bolognaise, and other Italian dishes.

PENNYROYAL

A less pungent type of mint, used in the same way, especially in fruit cups and other pleasant alcoholic drinks.

POT HERBS

An old-fashioned term denoting mixture of vegetables and herbs used for soup, sold cheaply under that name at greengrocers.

SAGE

Used in stuffing for meat and poultry, especially for roast goose. Try Sage Derby cheese. A Bouquet Garni herb.

TARRAGON

An aromatic herb with slight flavour of aniseed. Used with chicken, stews, salads and sauces, and to flavour vinegar, pickles.

JUNIPER

A member of the thyme family with light fresh flavour. Often used as substitute for ordinary lemon, and in stuffings.

MARJORAM

A more pungent member of the mint family. Used for soups, stews, fish, roast lamb. One of the herbs used in Bouquet Garni.

NASTURTIUM

The seeds are added to pickles, or used as a substitute for capers. The leaves and a few flowers can be added to salads.

PAPRIKA

Spicy rather than hot, made from large sweet red peppers (capsicum). Used in making tomato sauce, with chicken, Hungarian dishes.

PEPPERCORN

Black or white, ground to make pepper. Whole peppercorns are used in boiling meat for brawn or meat pies, for extra flavour.

ROSEMARY

The needle-like leaves improve roast beef and lamb, soups, stews, sauté potatoes, milk puddings, syllabub. Add a pinch to tea.

SAVORY

Has a delicate flavour of sage, used with cooked beans, soups, stews, and fresh or dried, for a different salad flavouring.

THYME

A Bouquet Garni herb, used in stuffing for meat, poultry and fish in soups and stews, and with many egg and tomato dishes.

Stalks are candied in the same way as angelica, have slight celery flavour. Scotch lovage is a vegetable, not a herb.

MINT

Very widely used, especially with lamb and veal, in ice-cream, fruit salad, custards, and in long cool summer drinks.

NUTMEG

The hard seed of the nutmeg tree after mace is stripped off, bought whole or as powder. Flavours sauces, desserts, cakes and biscuits.

PARSLEY

Used as a garnish, or chopped in sauces to serve with fish, boiled fowl, vegetables. Fry whole sprigs to accompany fried fish.

POPPY SEEDS

Fine grey opium-poppy seeds sprinkled on fancy bread rolls, cakes before baking, for decoration. Very mild in flavour.

SAFFRON

Orange-yellow stamens of the saffron crocus, sold in whole or powder form, used in cakes, savoury rice, bread to flavour and colour.

SORREL

Has a slightly acid flavour, and is used in sauces, salads and savouries, or as a puree with a number of meat or egg dishes.

TURMERIC

A bright yellow powdered root, aromatic and slightly bitter in flavour. A curry spice, also used in mustard pickles.

HERBS
for
COOKING
and for
HEALING

DONALD LAW
Ph.D., D.B.M., Dip.D., etc.

LONDON
W. FOULSHAM & CO. LTD.
NEW YORK . TORONTO . CAPETOWN . SYDNEY

W. FOULSHAM & CO. LTD.,
Yeovil Road, Slough, Bucks., England

PRINTED IN GREAT BRITAIN BY
BRISTOL TYPESETTING CO. LTD.

contents

meaning of words

In the second part of this book—*Herbs for Healing*—you will see that it has been necessary to use one or two words of a medical nature. To ensure that they cause as little confusion as possible, a list of their " definitions " is included below.

ANTHELMINTIC destroys parasitic worms.

ANTICONVULSANT alleviates and prevents fits and convulsions.

ANTISCORBUTIC a prevention of scurvy.

DERMATIC refers to the health of the skin.

DIURETIC promotes the discharge of urine.

EXPECTORANT clears the respiratory system.

EXPECTORATION spitting up.

FEBRIFUGE alleviates feverish conditions.

HAEMORRHOIDS the medical terms for piles.

LYMPHATIC SYSTEM the glandular system responsible for the body's defence against disease.

LYMPHATIC the fluids of the lymphatic system.

OPHTHALMIA inflammations of the eye.

PANACEA a supposed cure for all kinds of illness.

SILICA a mineral salt essential for the body.

SPECIFIC a medicine highly recommended to cure one's illness.

STAPHYLOCOCCI pus causing bacterial organisms.

STREPTOCOCCI another form of bacteria.

STYPTIC stops bleeding.

UVULA the small cone of flesh suspended from the top of the back of the mouth.

introduction

" Truth is the only daughter of Time " wrote the incomparable Leonardo da Vinci. Herbalism is as old as Man himself; it is not only the oldest of the healing arts, but still the safest—entirely free from the side-effects which render so many man-made drugs more dangerous than the disease.

The human body is the most remarkable combination of architecture, chemistry, engineering and physics in the whole universe; even an elementary grasp of any of the branches of knowledge specified when applied to the working of the human body reveals something of its wonders. " The body contains within itself the power to heal " wrote Hippocrates (460-377 B.C.). The whole theory of healing by medicinal herbs is based upon the art of helping the body to build up its own natural defences and restore good health, your natural birthright, by natural and wholesome methods.

Disease is not natural because it is a negative thing, it springs from Man's apathy, ignorance and neglect; it is true that many human beings spend more time and trouble caring for the cleanliness of their home than they spend caring for the cleanliness and efficiency of their bodies: Nobody would tolerate bad drains or broken windows in their houses for long, but it is surprising how many humans endure bodily discomfort, unnatural symptoms of pain for far too long before they go to a doctor.

Herbalism is basically a highly advanced form of dietetics. It introduces internally or externally substances which will build the body up, restore it and strengthen its natural defences. In the home we know that a leaky roof gets progressively worse if it is

neglected, and that as our mothers taught us " A stitch in time saves nine "—this must be your motto in caring for your health. Attend to any symptom of discomfort immediately you observe it; do not rush to take some highly advertised preparation which, by chemical means, promises to remove the pain. This does sound a little hard, but pain is only the barometer which tells us that we are under the weather physically, only when we have cured what *caused* the pain are we really well again.

Let me explain this another way. On the road there are some drivers who foolishly ignore the amber traffic light signal, instead of applying the brakes they depress the accelerator and try to beat the red light " Stop " signal: Many such drivers die young. This book has been written to help you live a long and healthy life and to enjoy every minute of it. Anybody who is ill obviously wants to get well as quickly as possible and generally speaking herbal medicine is not only very effective but also very quick acting; however, some conditions of long standing will take longer to clear up, conditions induced by long years of wrong living, wrong dietary habits and neglect can never be safely cured in a few days and people should be extremely wary of any preparation which (often at enormous expense) promises to do so.

This brings me to another point, herbal medicine is not only safer and older than other forms of medicine, it is also cheaper! Nearly all of the herbs you require for the most common illnesses can be grown in your own garden or flourish abundantly in the fields, woods and hedgerows of the countryside. This book includes a list of the herbs you can easily grow in your own garden or find in the countryside.

8

How do you know when you are really well again? This is another important question I am happy to answer. A complete cure is present when the patient feels consistently " on top of the world ". The disappearance of the symptoms does not mean that the underlying cause has been removed and disease cured: Nothing hinders the effectiveness of any treatment so much as the instantaneous abandonment of medicine and diet as soon as the symptoms first disappear.

You will notice that the herbalist never talks of " *killing* " germs to heal you. There has never been a medicine yet that is so perfectly selective that it destroys only the bad cells in the body and leaves the good, healthy cells unharmed: This is why herbalism—or *Botanic Medicine* as we tend to call it today, only talks of building up the body, restoring natural functions and strengthening you positively.

Clearly it is extremely important to identify the plants you use, especially because when you need them you may not have them in stock and may have to buy them from a shop selling herbs, therefore by the side of each plant named I give its Latin name by which it can be identified throughout the world. Supposing you wanted the plant we commonly call Dandelion, in France it is Piss-en-lit, in Germany it is Löwenzahn, in Sweden it is Maskros and in Yugoslavia it is called Maslachak—but in every country if you ask for *Taraxacum officinalis* you will get the simple Dandelion you need. There is yet another reason why you must *always quote the Latin name if you buy herbs from a dealer,* it is that the popular folk names of herbs in England and America are confusing; for example " Periwinkle " in England is the *Vinca major,* but the plant they call " Periwinkle " in America is the

Gaultheria procumbens, and they have quite different uses.

You will be not a little surprised to learn that many of the plants you looked upon as " weeds " are in fact extremely valuable medical plants. Emerson once said : — " A weed is a plant whose virtues we have not yet discovered ".

Be careful never to spray any herbs with any chemical sprays, you would do more harm than good. I recommend Rachel Carson's world famous book " The Silent Spring " to all readers, it will give you eloquent reasons not to use any sprays or chemical weedkillers.

This book will not enable you to become a herbalist but it will enable you to use herbs safely to alleviate many common ills, pains and suffering : Be careful to use them exactly as recommended. Never, and I repeat, never add to the doses or alter the recipes unless so advised by a qualified practitioner of Botanic Medicine; it is totally wrong to believe that you can speed up a cure by increasing the dose of the medicine or by increasing its quantity.

In closing this introduction I will leave you with these thoughts—most of us know when we are ill, few know when they are well—it is easier to preserve health than to recover it—or in Shakespeare's words : " Self-love is not so vile a sin as self-neglecting ".

In the firm belief that this knowledge will keep you well and help you restore health I have written this book for you.

Donald Law,

Ph.D., D.B.M., Dip.D.

how to identify and collect herbs

It is possible to purchase nearly all the herbs described in this book from any of the innumerable Health Shops, Herbal Suppliers or *Reformhaus* in any civilized country, but for those who like to go out and collect their own I am adding some useful advice.

Many herbals offer a brief description of the plants described; as a practitioner of Botanic Medicine I have rarely found these descriptions adequate; that an amateur or a novice should collect herbs without a precise knowledge as to what he is collecting is unthinkable. There are some 12,000 species of Compositae, and it is clearly beyond the scope of this handbook to list details to look out for to distinguish one variety from another.

Luckily there are a good many most useful books published with coloured illustrations and exact descriptions which make identification simple. I recommend the purchase of one of these books which I find helpful in my own country walks when I am gaining health by searching for the herbs which will keep me in health during the winter months.

Once you have identified the herbs that you want, there are certain rules which a successful herb-gatherer is recommended to follow. Most of them are commonsense when you stop to think about them.

I   Never take all the leaves or all the flowers from any one plant; you could kill the plant and endanger further supplies in future years. I make it a rule to take not more than a quarter of its

11

leaves or heads from any single plant. Other herbalists may come along after you—and your combined efforts could kill the plant. The Poles had a quaint custom when collecting flowers—their saying was " Always leave some for God."

II   Try to collect your herbs at their best period, not when they are too young, but before they are too old; your sight and sense will guide you in many cases but do not hesitate to consult the botany identification books if in doubt.

III   Herbs collected with dew or rain upon them may easily turn mouldy and lose all virtue within a few hours. Collect them in dry paper bags, you can keep the herbs in them more easily because they are slightly absorbent; the bags can be carried in polythene holders.

IV   Try not to crush the plants when travelling home : a crushed plant is a dying plant, and you will lose some of its medical value.

V   Never mix all your herbs together when they have been picked; within an hour or so they will be doubly hard to identify.

VI   Generally you collect the top parts of a herb if you seek the leaf or the flower.

VII   Take the greatest care not to collect herbs that have been sprayed with agricultural chemicals, or are covered with dust or petrol fumes. If in doubt leave them; there are many alternatives in Botanic Medicine.

VIII   Avoid leaves which are mottled or obviously host to insects.

IX   For flowers make certain that they are freshly opened and do not carry insects.

X   In the case of the bark or roots being collected take good care to wash these thoroughly and dry them slowly. If you take bark remember that the bark of a slender stick is better than the bark off of the mother tree!

how to dry herbs

Now here, in simplified form, are the rules about drying herbs. It is not widely known that the modern word *drug* comes from the Anglo Saxon word for dried herbs, although the modern often treacherous, artificial preparations have no relationship with the safe and simple herbal medicines with thousands of years of remedies behind them.

1 When you reach home with your herbs, clear a kitchen table or similar wide surface, cover it with clean brown paper or lining paper. Wash the herbs in a bowl of pure water, lay them out on your prepared table, then proceed as follows:—

   (a) If you are hanging them up to dry in a *really dry* room tie them round with string in small bunches; do not make thick bundles or drying will be slow and mildew most likely set in. Natural drying takes 4 to 6 weeks.

   (b) If you are going to oven-dry them see note 2 below.

2 In our damp British climate it is hardly feasible to dry herbs by hanging them up in a room and expecting them to dry perfectly without help. Put a layer of strong brown paper in your oven, spread the herbs *thinly* across the paper, and leave the oven on the lowest possible gas or electricity heating. This means you can bottle and store the herbs within a few hours of collection, and it saves a lot of trouble. There is one insuperable argument in favour of this method, none of your herbs should ever go mildew.

3　You will know when your herbs are " done " because they will be completely crisp, dry, not too brittle, and will still retain their colour. *Never leave them to bake brown!* If leaves do misfortunately bake brown because you left them in the oven too long, throw them away, they are useless. Flowers should retain something of their natural colour. Barks and roots may turn fairly dark upon oven-drying, do not worry about them. Powder the bark before storing it; you can use a kitchen grater for this.

4　When the herbs are dried crumble them up, or use a mincing machine and keep them in a brown, lightproof bottle. The bottles must have a screwtop lid and be kept as airtight as possible. Dried herbs will last for several years, keeping their potency all the time.

herbs you can grow at home

If you have a large garden you can easily set aside one corner of it to grow herbs. Pay a visit to any of the great Botanical Gardens, and you will see how pretty a herb garden can be. When growing herbs in your garden do read books on plant identification, and do take care to transplant herbs, or plant seeds only in the conditions under which they grow naturally. If the plant normally grows in shade, keep it planted in the shade, if it needs damp and you have a very dry soil, don't try to grow it. *No plant will produce the same beneficial results if it does not grow in its own preferred natural conditions.*

For those who have to live in a flat there is still an opportunity to grow herbs in pots or window boxes, but a word of warning here, do make sure that the container is really big enough for the roots to develop. Those that can be grown indoors are marked with an asterisk *.

Agrimony (Agrimonia eupatoria)
Alder tree (Alnus glutinosa)
All Heal (Stachys sylvatica)
Anemone (Anemone nemorosa)
Archangel (Archangelica umbelliferae)
Asparagus (Asparagus officinalis)
Aspen tree (Populus tremula)

Balm (Melissa officinalis)*
Barley (Hordeum pratense)
Beans (Faba)
Beech tree (Fagus sylvatica)

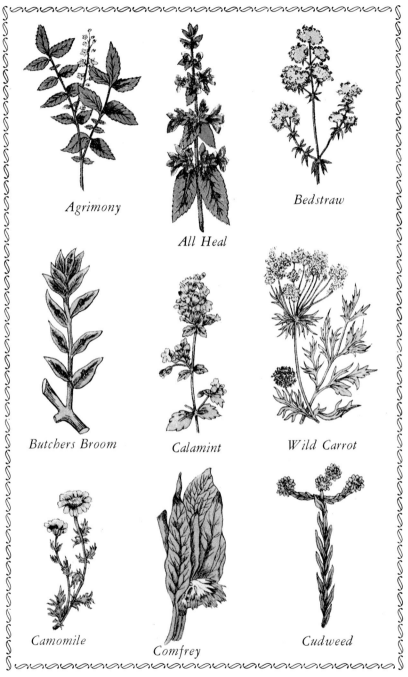

Agrimony

All Heal

Bedstraw

Butchers Broom

Calamint

Wild Carrot

Camomile

Comfrey

Cudweed

Betony

Brook Lime

Burnet Saxifrage

Burnet

Bistort

Buckbean

Bergamot (Monarda fistulosa)*
Bilberry (Vaccinium myrtillus)
Birch tree (Betula pendula)
Blackberry (Rubus fructicosus)
Broom (Spartium scoparium)
Burnet (Sanguisorba minor)

Camomile (Anthemis nobilis)
Carrot (Daucus carota)
Celandine (Chelidonum majus)
Celery (Apium graveolens)
Cherry (Cerasus duracina)
Chervil (Anthriscus cerefoliata)*
Chestnut tree (Castanea vulgaris)
Horse Chestnut tree (Aesculus hippocastanum)
Chickweed (Stellaria media)*
Cinquefoil (Potentilla reptans)*
Clary (Salvia sclarea)
Clover, red (Trifolium pratense)
Colts Foot (Tussilago farfara)
Columbines (Aquilegia vulgaris)
Comfrey (Symphytum officinalis)
Cowslip (Primula veris)

Daffodils (Narcissus pseudonarcissus)*
Dandelion (Taxacum officinalis)
Dock, red (Rumex aquaticus)

Elder bush (Sambucus nigra)
Elecampane (Inula viscosa)
Eyebright (Euphrasia officinalis)

Fennel (Foeniculum officinale)
Fenugreek (Trigonella foenum graecum)

B

Flax (Linum usitatissimum)
Fleabane (Erigeron canadensis)
Frog Bit (Hydrocaris morus ranae)
Fumitory (Fumaria officinalis)

Gentian (Gentiana campestris)
Golden Rod (Solidago odora)
Groundsel (Senecio vulgaris)

Hawthorn bush (Crateagus monogyna)
Heartsease (Viola tricolor)*
Heather (Ericaceae)
Hoarhound (Marrubium vulgare)
Hollyhock (Althea rosa)
Hops (Humulus lupulus)
Horsetail Grass (Equisetum arvense)

Icelandic Moss (Cetraria islandica)
Ivy (Hedera helix)

Lavender (Lavandula vera)
Leadwort (Plumbago europaea)

Marigold (Calendula officinalis)*
Marjoram (Origanum vulgare)
Medlar tree (Mespilus germanica)
Mellitot (Melitotus officinalis)
Mint (Mentha viridis)*

Nettle (Urtica dioica)

Onion (Allium cepa)

Parsley (Petroselium sativum)*

Pine tree (Pinus sylvestris)
Potato (Solanum tuberosum)

Raspberry (Rubus idaeus)
Dog Rose (Rosa canina)

Sage (Salvia officinalis)*
St. John's Wort (Hypericum perforatum)
Silverweed (Potentilla anserina)
Speedwell (Veronica officinalis)
Sycamore tree (Acer pseudoplatanus)

Tansy (Tanacetum vulgare)
Thyme (Thymus vulgaris)

Vervain (Verbena officinalis)
Violet (Viola odorata)

Wallflowers (Cheiranthus cheiri)

Yarrow (Achillea millefolium)

cooking with herbs

In all of the most tasty and elegant forms of cooking, the use of culinary herbs is absolutely essential.

The amazing range of variations which can be obtained from the use of single or mixed herbs accounts for the gamut of dishes and wines (often spiced!) throughout the world.

The important rule to remember is that you must never drown your dish in flavouring, one of the great charms of Japanese and Chinese *cuisines* is the subtlety of taste which is employed; if you cannot eat oriental food slowly you had better eat fish and chips instead. If you are ever in a restaurant and the dish is very heavily flavoured you had better send it away, the cook must be trying to hide some fault! Herbs which are particularly strong in their effect are marked with a dagger symbol [†].

Now a second rule to bring your dishes their well-deserved success. Do not put your flavouring herbs into the dish at the beginning of the cooking process, only add them about thirty minutes before you take them off the heating, out of the oven etc. The sole exception is, of course, the omelette! My father always reigned supreme in our house as the only maker of omelettes: My mother could cook everything else magnificently, but for omelettes we always turned to father who had an exceptional gift for mixing a pinch of this, a *soupçon of that*. Keep all your herbs handy when you are making an omelette, and remember that a " pinch " signifies as much of the herb as you can take between a forefinger and thumb!

ALLSPICE

Try this with beetroot, cabbage, corned beef, most meat roasts, potatoes, spaghetti. Some people use it with apples and pears.

ANGELICA

The fresh green leaves are rather nice with white fish.

ANISE

The dry seeds are quite attractive in bread and cakes. The fresh leaves can be chopped up fine in soups.

BASIL

Its name comes from the Greek word for king, and hence the plant has been called the " royal " herb. Poultry, salads, sausages, spaghetti, and your afternoon cup of tea can all be bettered by the judicious addition of Basil.

BAY†

Fish, Pickles, Salads, Stews and stuffing all will taste new and exciting if you add a touch of Bay. Try one leaf only with your custard!

BERGAMOT

A favourite herb of my learned friend Dr. Thomas, astronomer and historian, who taught me to use it. This is the " Oswego Tea " referred to in the early novels of the *frontier* life by Fenimore Cooper and others. Apart from making it as an individual tea you can add it to ordinary black tea or to salads.

BORAGE

Add a little to your lemonade, lemon-barley, orangeade, allow it to stand for a quarter of an hour —you'll love it.

BURNET

This is often called " Salad Burnet " so you can mix it with salads, particularly salads containing cucumber and tomato or potato.

CALAMUS

This comes from the orient, it is a rather more delicate aroma than ginger, and makes a good ginger substitute in cakes, bread, or puddings.

CAMOMILE

You can make a nice soothing tea or add some dried flowers to the ordinary tea you prepare.

CAPERS

Veal cutlets, veal stew, rabbit and pork can be garnished with caper sauce.

CARAWAY

If you have never had caraway bread, or what my old trapper uncle called " old seedy cake " you have never lived! Many of the Danish country cheeses are liberally sprinkled with caraway. Try adding a few seeds to pork, goulashes, stews or *mashed potatoes and cream*!

CARDAMONS

These seeds are really a trifle exotic, but you just see what happens when you sprinkle a few over your jellies, cakes, pastries, biscuits (in the last fifteen minutes only). Your family will raid your larder until all are gone!

CAYENNE

One of the familiar household peppers. Some people are a little too liberal with it, stick to egg dishes, fish and the occasional salad when you're handing this out.

CELERY SEED

This does something for your sauceboat, gravies and stews. Pickles and potatoes taste nice, especially in winter, if you use celery seeds. You can make a tonic tea for yourself from them.

CHERVIL

Cheeses and soups.

CHILLIES†

An extraordinary rich source of Vitamin C. With salads, with meats, stews, with roast steak (last fifteen minutes; with all kinds of sauces).

CHIVES

Friends of mine in Copenhagen use them almost daily on their *Smørrebrød;* try them with cheese sandwiches, white fish (add after serving), add to salads, soups (after serving) and to fried eggs.

CICELY

Try this with potatoes, rolls, or sauces. It is often called " Sweet Cicely " so do not expect it to be bitter.

CINNAMON

I make cinnamon bread and rolls, I add it to cakes, to milk puddings, to tea (in the Arab fashion); take some cinnamon in your hot milk with a little honey when you retire for the night.

CLARY

Add to soups, to home made wines or serve chopped fine with cheese sandwiches.

CLOVES†

This is the strange taste in so many of those wonderful German and Swiss biscuits and cakes which they give their guests at Christmas time. Flavour the tea with a couple of cloves (not more), especially if you've got a cold. You can add cloves to apples or to pears when stewing them. My father's father loved pears intently, and liked them slightly flavoured with cloves.

CORIANDER

Many years ago I was very friendly with a pretty Greek nurse, and from her I learnt to use coriander seeds. You can use them with cakes and pastries, with bread rolls, with olives and in stews.

CURRY†

Too much is not good for those who are unused to it. Please don't be heavy-handed when wielding a spoon with curry in it. Although many are inclined to add curry to all sorts of dishes, my advice is to keep it for rice dishes or mixed vegetables. And if you have a weak liver do not indulge too frequently.

26

DILL

Cheese dishes, pickles, salads; boiled potatoes (during last ten minutes), *consommes*, and white fish.

ELDER

The flowers have many medicinal uses, and can also be added to a tea when you feel tired or feverish.

FENNEL

One of the very finest of herbal teas, especially if your tummy is tired or upset. A good tonic. You can add them to several fish dishes, to pickles, gravies and sauces.

FENUGREEK†

You can add a few to gravies, to stews or some dishes like tripe which is a little insipid alone.

GARLIC†

You will find that many of the best cooks merely rub the cut clove of garlic around the pot in which a dish is to be prepared and then throw the clove away, which indicates how strong it is! Nevertheless as this is one of the most highly beneficial medicinal plants to man it seems unthankful to treat garlic so ungratefully, when you cast it away do remember that it will act as a disinfectant and antiseptic, and even a once used piece of garlic slung away from the kitchen can still serve you. Soups and meat dishes mainly, especially with some mutton dishes. If you venture to add a little to salads, make sure it is a little, unless you are taking it for medicinal reasons. If your family object to the smell of garlic, ensure that all have just a little, then nobody will detect it in the others. In

27

many countries where horsemeat is served, they employ garlic to disguise the natural sweetness of this flesh. I strongly advise against using it with any poultry.

GINGER†

We all know how to flavour bread, cakes, pies, puddings, and rolls with it, but how many use it like my grandmother did to flavour fruit? Apple tart with a touch of ginger is something to write home about. I lived with Cantonese Chinese who used ginger to flavour chicken, and sometimes rice as well.

HOARHOUND†

In the lifetime of my grandmother's mother this was sometimes used to add taste to home-made fudge. I think you had better try it in a really old-fashioned stew the first time you use it, or maybe a sauce. It makes a pleasant tea alone or can be added to Indian tea; it is a useful tonic in this form.

HORSERADISH

There is nothing to match a home-made horse-radish sauce with a mouthwatering dish of roast beef; I do not care for factory prepared sauces. Some cooks use it with tuna and other fish, but I cannot honestly recommend it myself.

HYSSOP

This is quite a different taste to put into your casseroles and goulashes. It is but one of the herbs mentioned in the Bible, so men have enjoyed it for centuries.

28

JUNIPER†

In olden times it was the fashion to use the berries with venison or pork.

LAVENDER†

The flowers are used to make wonderful sachets to scent our linen cupboards. A great aunt of mine, famed for her wit and intellect, used to make the most beautifully ornamented net and tulle sachets of fresh lavender to give to us all at Christmas. Try a few of the flowers in a cup of tea next time you feel tired after the housework. You can try just a little lavender flower in with some mashed potatoes.

LEMON BALM

In tea, a drink alone with hot water and brown sugar (quite refreshing); use it to perfume your clothes cupboards. Try a little chopped up in the salad.

LOVAGE

This can be added to cold chopped meat dishes.

MACE

Somewhat over used in oriental cuisine, it is not widely known in the West. Mix a little in with sausage meat or with meat-balls, *frickadella,* kofta, or if feeling very daring sprinkle a *soupçon* of mace over blancmange or any milk pudding.

MARIGOLD

Apart from many medical uses, it makes a refreshing tea especially if you have been having heart troubles, palpitations, etc. Sprinkle some fresh leaves of the flower on your summer lunchtime salads: The result is both appetizing and pretty.

MARJORAM

There is probably no other herb which suits lamb so well; you may try it with roast duck as well. I am very partial to marjoram in a rich vegetable stew where there are plenty of leeks or onions.

MINT

There are many varieties of mint but all of them can be used with potatoes; most of them go well with salads. An old fashioned mint sauce with pure vinegar is marvellous with any roast dish of fatty meat, especially lamb. I do advise you to cultivate your own mint and make your own mint sauce; when I was a lad that was one of my chores on a Sunday, we used only mint, vinegar and brown sugar.

MUGWORT

When I was studying at Heidelberg I had a remarkable supper once with one of the lecturers, the goose was flavoured with this herb which they call *Berifuss*; Germans maintain that this is good against catarrh of the stomach. The plant is related to that from which the drink Vermouth is prepared.

MUSTARD

A great aid to digestion if you are having meat.

NASTURTIUM

The chopped leaves will make your salads famous.

NIGELLA

A dear friend of mine in Versailles uses the seeds instead of poppy seeds to sprinkle on her oven-fresh rolls.

30

NUTMEG

Time permitting I like nothing better than to bake a cake and I hardly ever do so without a most liberal helping of nutmeg (put it in as the very last ingredient). I have also added it to home-made bread (use less nutmeg); Custard and all milk dishes benefit by a pinch of nutmeg. Try it on pears or stewed apples.

OREGANO

You'd better try to get the Mexican variety if you want to flavour fried beans, pasta dishes (spaghetti, vermicelli, etc.) or your soup with oregano.

PAPRIKA

In my youth I was greatly taken by an attractive Hungarian emigrée countess (she said she was), all that remains is a predilection for paprika! I like paprika-flavoured cheese and paprika with salads. Try it with roast meats too. It is one of the richest sources of Vitamin C in Europe.

PARSLEY

One of the most valuable and nutritious herbs on this planet. If in doubt add parsley to any salad, stew, potatoes, fish, or omelettes. It is also one of the most attractive decorations to food on the table.

PEPPER

Frankly I feel it is one of the most overused and abused of all spices. Vary your peppers, there are several. And do not fly to them too often. I heard of a case where a very deep knife wound stopped bleeding completely after a dressing of pepper.

31

POPPY

The seeds are used to sprinkle on bread, cakes and rolls. The famous *Linzertorte* is mainly made of them.

ROSEMARY

The herb that symbolizes remembrance can make your pilaf, veal, and ham dishes quite memorable. Don't be too heavy handed if you use it in sauces.

RUE†

Slightly bitter, but you may like it in gravy and stews.

SAFFRON

Formerly a favourite ingredient of pastries and cakes (do you remember saffron buns?), but it is rather difficult to find nowadays. Cheese and meat were also sometimes spiced with saffron, I am not sure that this is a universal taste, so try it first in buns or biscuits.

SAGE

Sucking-pigs, turkey, and ham are nice with sage; veal will take it—but not too much! A tonic tea on its own.

One old English cheese is flavoured with sage.

SAVORY

Frequently employed to liven up dishes such as lentils, beans, boiled greens, potatoes. Very popular in Switzerland. I have not met it much outside of Central Europe, but it is quite attractive. *(Satureia hortensis)*.

SORREL

Chop up the fresh leaves for your salads.

32

TANSY

Try making some real old English Tansy cakes, do not be worried if they assume a rich yellowish colour. Our forefathers loved them.

TARRAGON

I believe this takes its name from that ancient and lovely city that many visitors to eastern Spain know and like. I used to prepare rump steak with tarragon and a little wine, delicious! I eat meat very rarely, so when I do partake I like to make it really tasty. Poultry, fish, salads and stews can be rendered mouth-watering delicacies by using this herb.

THYME

They say that this herb will flavour any meat, poultry, fish or vegetable dish. Don't overdo it! We used to put it in bags of cottage cheese hung up to " cheesify " when I was a boy. It is a most beautiful aromatic herb to grow " I know a bank where the wild thyme grows " says Shakespeare. I like it as a tea with a little brown sugar. It is a very effective vermifuge should you have been eating fruit which you subsequently discover to have maggots.

TURMERIC

An Indian spice, highly coloured and very rich in taste. While a little knowledge is a dangerous thing, too much turmeric is definitely too much. Go easy with it!

first aid in the kitchen

Many housewives know that accidents always happen when you have least time to deal with them, and many precious minutes can be lost in rushing round to the chemist for some expensive pharmaceutical preparation to heal the hurt.

It is an incontrovertible fact that many substances commonly found in a kitchen are of botanic origin and have valuable medicinal properties in them. In this section of the book I am listing some of the conditions which you can deal with without moving from the kitchen at all.

GENERAL WARNING

All the remedies suggested in this section of the book are essentially for emergency use and do not replace any of the medicinal herbs recommended in the main section.

ACIDITY IN THE STOMACH

Sip a dessertspoonful of raw potato juice.

ASTHMATIC ATTACK

A dessertspoonful of honey in three dessertspoonfuls of applecider vinegar with a cupful of warm water.

BOILS

Either a fresh slice of onion or a covering of lint soaked in raw potato juice. In either case cover with an adhesive dressing, after applying treatment.

Great Celandine

Little Celandine

Cat Mint

Centaury

Corn Marigold

Cranesbill

Chickweed

Colt's Foot

Crosswort

Red Darnel

Devil's Bit

Dropwort

Eyebright

Earthnut

Eryngo

BRUISE
Apply a slice of fresh beetroot, then hold it in position with adhesive plasters.

BURNS
Mint leaves or raw potato juice, then cover with clean, dry lint; keep it on with plasters.

CATARRH
Gargle with salt and water, or with cinnamon and water. Inhale over a bowl of hot water surrounding this with a towel, in the water you can put a little cinnamon or some eucalyptus.

CHAPS
Apply raw potato juice.

CHILBLAINS
Apple or potato juice. Try cucumber juice.

COLDS
See the medical section for detailed information, but for the emergency take some drinks of pure lemon juice, honey and warm water.

CONSTIPATION
Dessertspoonful of honey in warm water taken first thing on rising.

CORNS
Paint with lemon juice, or apply a freshly cut clove of garlic. In either case cover with lint and hold on with adhesive plaster.

DEPRESSION
A good cup of tea, a mustard bath for those tired feet, and turn the radio on!

DIARRHOEA
Arrowroot mixed with milk, one to three dessert-spoonfuls.

EYESTRAIN
Apple juice or the liquid from boiled apples mixed half and half with cold water, apply in an eyebath.

FAINTING
Beetroot juice, a lemon juice and honey drink, a rosemary tea will help.

FEET TIRED
A mustard bath; rub with applecider vinegar, or rub gently with lemon juice. Pinecones bath.

HEADACHE
This may be a sign of a chill so look under "colds". Make a nice cup of thyme tea! Mint leaves applied to the temples will relieve you.

HOARSE THROAT
A gargle of sage and vinegar may help.

INDIGESTION
Fennel tea is very mild and helpful.

INFLUENZA
Honey, lemon and cinnamon in warm water.

INSECT BITES

Witch hazel or lemon juice or a slice of onion all very helpful, especially the last.

JOINTS, STIFF

Pour boiling water over some pine cones. When only lukewarm bathe the joints with it. Otherwise a light massage with corn oil, olive oil or sunflower oil.

LIVER UPSET

Lemon juice and water. A little applecider vinegar and water.

NERVOUS UPSET

Make a tea of sage, of thyme or of rosemary. Beetroot juice will help.

NOSE BLEEDING

Put some witch hazel on a little clean piece of cloth or cottonwool and then plug the nose. Only do this if the bleeding is very severe, much nosebleeding stops in time without help.

PALPITATIONS

Treat as for nervous upset.

POISONING

Check with expert advice immediately. Treatment varies according as to whether the poisoning is of acid or alkali origin. General rules are as follows: — Do whatever possible to *dilute the poison* by giving the patient drinks which are also emetic in nature; the body will usually vomit up considerable quantities of

39

a poison if given half a chance. DO NOT GIVE AN EMETIC IF ALKALIS OR STRONG ACIDS HAVE BEEN SWALLOWED, the stomach would most likely be damaged under the strain of being sick. The patient should be persuaded to drink from five to seven tumblers of a diluting liquid, milk and water, or water alone, if possible a very thin gruel with millet or oatflakes in it may help protect the delicate internal tissues. If *Alkali, Ammonia, Caustic Acid,* or *lye* have been swallowed you can give lemon juice to aid recovery. If it should be *arsenic* you may administer castor oil. *Acetic acid, benzine, hydrochloric acid,* are rendered less toxic by taking quantities of vegetable oils. The taking of quantities of milk will minimise the effects of *acetic acid, chlorinated lime, chromium trioxide, copper sulphate, hydrofluoric acid, lead,* or *silversalts.*

FOOD POISONING

Rule one : If you think you have eaten food which you subsequently notice to be mouldy or attacked by fungus, or drink milk from a tin later found to be unclean, take some applecider vinegar in water.

Rule two : Shellfish poisoning, take castor oil quickly, rest in bed, keep the patient warm and give natural stimulants. Call doctor, and give as much warm water as the patient will drink.

Rule three : Mushroom poisoning, call a doctor; flush out the system with warm water.

Rule four : Tinned food poisoning, wash out system with lots of warm water and a teaspoonful of applecider vinegar in every second tumbler of water. Do call a doctor.

Rule five : Salmonella or Ptomaine poisoning. Call an expert as quickly as possible. No food at all. The patient must vomit, administer as much warm water as the patient will drink; apply warmth to the stomach.

SORE THROAT
Sage tea.

TEETH & GUMS
Rub lemon peel over them gently, it will strengthen and clean. Lemon peel has a lot of Vitamins C & P, which will keep your mouth healthy.

TOOTHACHE
Clove powder or oil of cloves.

VARICOSE VEINS
Apply a little cooling witch hazel for quick relief.

VOMITING
Either lemon juice or applecider vinegar in water.

recipes for herbal treatments

Writing my paper on the "Problems of Diagnosis" I began it with this sentence: "In all branches of healing the greatest problem is that of diagnosis; the more exactly the practitioner of healing can define the condition the easier and speedier the possibilities of cure become".

The following works will be of considerable help to you in diagnosing, with reasonable accuracy, various conditions. Black's Medical Dictionary, Red Cross and St. John's Handbook of First Aid, The Natural Home Physician by Eric Powell, Ph.D., M.D., Elementary Anatomy and Physiology published by Churchills, and finally Messrs. Bailliers Tindall and Cox publish a series of booklets which nurses and students frequently use.

When your diagnosis has been made, you can refer to the complaint in our index on page 47. This will direct you to the herbs that will be of benefit. You can then refer to a particular herb, where instructions on its administration will be given.

To save a great deal of space and repetition the various *recipes* are printed here, so that when making up your preparations you will probably need to come back to this page.

DECOCTION : —

1 Take one ounce of the indicated herb *unless otherwise recommended*, and boil up in one pint of water. If a smaller quantity of herb is indicated do **NOT** exceed that amount. Generally boil the mixtures slowly, never boil them quickly.

2 Never boil them in aluminium, use only copper or enamel saucepans. Aluminium is a very toxic substance, anybody who wishes to read up on the subject might study *Aluminium, a Menace to Health* by Mark Clement.

OINTMENTS : —
1 You require 4 ozs. of the herb (dried)
         6 ozs. Coconut fat.
         1 oz. Beeswax.
2 Melt the coconut fat, stir in all ingredients, leave for one to one and a half hours over a low heat. At the end of this time, pour out into cleaned containers.
3 Ointments retain their strength for about two years.

POULTICE : —
1 These can be made from fresh or dried herbs, they draw out poisons and soothe.
2 Spread the herb on a piece of clean lint or bandage either hot or cold, as required. Cold poultices are Slower in effect than hot. Remember to test with your elbow to feel how hot a poultice is before you apply it.

HERBAL TEAS : —
1 Put from one to three teaspoonfuls of herb in a family sized teapot, pour on boiling water and leave it to infuse for ten minutes, then drink as ordinary tea.
2 Never use white sugar, only use honey or brown sugar as sweetening agents. See my book on *Herbal Teas for Health and Pleasure.*

43

NOTE: Never expect an illness to clear away after only a few days of medication; some illnesses take weeks to appear and will take at least a week or two to disappear. Occasionally you will see an almost immediate improvement, but keep taking the treatment until you feel on top of the world again.

maladies and herbs

In this list it is understood that cure and alleviation of any illness depends upon the efficiency of the diagnosis.

In several illnesses self-medication is not advisable unless there is no alternative available, among these are: Cancer, Diabetes, Erysipelas, Gangrene, Gonorrhoea, some severe arthritic and rheumatic conditions, Tuberculosis, Typhus, and Venereal diseases. Our ancestors were treated for these by experienced herbalists, and many experienced and well qualified practitioners of Botanic Medicine are still available for consultation. Personally I use *only* botanic and dietetic healing for the care of my own health.

The list given here is only presented as a handy guide and the full text of the book must be examined for further details.

Abcesses	Lemon
Acidity	Mellitot
Anaemia	Blackberry, Nettle, Raspberry
Antiscorbutic	Brooklime
Antiseptics	Garlic, Onion, Lemon, Cinnamon
Acne (Pimples)	Devil's Bit
Arthritis	Catmint, Garlic, Nettle, Sea-brack
Asthma	Agrimony

Biliousness	Fluxweed
Bites	Parsley
Bladder conditions	Asparagus, Betony, Irish Moss,
Bladder stones	Birch, Dropwort
Blood fevers	Garlic

Blood cleanser	Clover (Red), Dandelion, Speedwell
Boils	Mullein, Tansy
Bone knitting	Comfrey, Fluxweed
Breast swelling	Beans
Bruising (Internal)	Sage, Figwort
Burns	Potato, St. John's Wort, Alder
Cancer	Clover (Red), Violet, Watercress
Carbuncles	Tansy, Lemon
Catarrh	Bilberry, Blackberry, Garlic
Cardiac (condition)	Hawthorn, Hollyhock
Cataract	Clary
Chapped skin	Groundsel
Chilblains	Adders Tongue
Cholesterol	Hawthorn, Hollyhock
Childbirth	Raspberry
Colic	Thyme, Kummel
Complexion	Elder, Beech
Constipation	See Laxatives
Corns	Dandelion
Convulsions	Heartsease
Coughs	Blackberry, Cherry, Coltsfoot
Cramp	Calamint
Cysts	Watercress
Colds	Bilberry, Blackberry, Elder
Cuts	Carrot (wild)
Depression	Ginger
Dermatic	Dandelion, Beech
Diabetes	Beech, Bistort, Carrot, Dandelion, Lemon
Diarrhoea	Blackberry, Fluxweed, Silverweed
Digestion	Fluxweed, Golden Rod
Disinfectant	Lemon
Dropsy	Alder, Asparagus, Birch, Buckbean, Hawthorn, Nettle, Tansy

Dysentery	Avens, Balm, Lemon, St. John's Wort
Diuretic	Birch
Earache	Horsetail Grass
Eczema	Elder, Golden Rod, Marigold
Epilepsy	Heartsease
Exhaustion	Fluxweed
Eye lotions	Elder, Eyebright, Adders Tongue, Clary
Eye troubles	Speedwell, Watercress, Flag, Honeywort
Eye watering	Beans
Expectoration	Archangel
Eye cataract	Clary
Erysipelas	Chickweed, Golden Rod, Lemon, Marigold
Febrifuge	Centaury, Aspen
Female Complaints	Camomile, Hollyhock, Motherwort, Feverfew
Fertility	Mint, Sage
Fibrositis	Watercress
Flu	Yarrow
Fevers	Avens, Balm, Fleabane, Tansy
Fleas	Fleabane
Fractures	Comfrey, Fluxweed
Freckles	Cowslip
Gall stones	Broom
Gangrene	Alder
Gargle	Bistort
Genitals	Golden Seal
Gland Swelling	Buckbean, Cudweed, Ivy
Gonorrhoea	Butcher's Broom
Gout	Goutwort, Birch
Gum weakness	Buckbean, Lemon
Haemorrhoids	Catmint, Corn-marigold, Dandelion, Houndstongue

Hayfever	Elecampane
Hangovers	Marjoram
Heartburn	Archangel
Heart conditions	Motherwort,
Hernia	Crosswort, Comfrey
Hysteria	Bedstraw, Camomile
Hydrophobia	Chickweed
Indigestion	Archangel, Burnet Saxifrage
Insomnia	Cowslip
Impotence	Balm
Jaundice	Agrimony, Asparagus, Cinquefoil, Columbine, Corn-marigold, St. John's Wort
Kidney conditions	Asparagus, Betony, Birch, Dodder of Thyme, Golden Rod, Irish Moss
Kidney (ulcerated)	Cinquefoil
Liver complaints	Broom, St. John's Wort, Tansy
Liver obstruction	Columbine, Harts Tongue
Leucorrhoea	Avens
Lumbago	Pimpernel, Watercress
Laryngitis	Garlic
Laxative (Gentle)	Dandelion, Liquorice
Laxative (Strong)	Hoarhound
Lymphatic	Asparagus, Dandelion
Measles	Corn Marigold
Menstruation (heavy)	Silverweed
Menstruation (painful)	Centaury, Cinquefoil, Fennel
Miscarriage (prevention)	Medlar
Mumps	Cudweed

48

Muscle Sprain or Strain	Daffodils, Marigold
Muscle Ache	Calamint
Nervous complaints	Balm, Barley, Bedstraw, Bergamot,
Nose bleeding	Camomile, Vervain, Oats
Obesity	Nettle, Sea-wrack
Oral complaints	Buck bean
Perspiration	Hares Foot
Pharyngitis	Cherry, Garlic
Piles	Catmint, Horse chestnut, witch-hazel
Pimples	Devils Bit
Pneumonia	Liquorice, Yarrow
Poisoned stings	Balm, Parsley
Pregnancy (during)	Fenugreek
Pregnancy (sickness)	Marjoram
Purgative	Broom
Rectal Infection	Horse chestnut
Respiratory complaints	Irish Moss, Kummel, Liquorice
Rickets	Icelandic Moss, Watercress
Rheumatic complaints	Betony, Birch, Catmint, Cranesbill, Ivy, Nettle, Potato, Sea-wrack, Yarrow
Ringworms	Catmint, Liverwort
Sciatica	Juniper, Nettle
Scalp	Lemon
Sedatives	Hops
Senility	Balm
Sexual organs— cleansing	Witch-hazel
Shock	Sage
Sinus trouble	Elecampane

49

Skin blemishes	Cowslip, Marigold
Skin troubles	Agrimony, Beech
Sleeplessness (insomnia)	Camomile, Hops
Sores	Carrot (wild)
Splinters	Darnel (Red)
Stings	Parsley
Stress	Sage
St. Vitus Dance	Cowslip
Styes	Chickweed, Tansy
Styptic	Jacinth
Testicle Swelling	Beans
Tetanus	Mountain Holly
Thorns	Gladrom
Toothache	Leadwort
Tonics	Centaury, Golden Rod, Lemon, Wallflower
Tranquillizers	Cowslip
Throat Infection	Bilberry, Blackberry
Tuberculosis	Colts Foot, Liquorice
Typhus	Onion, Garlic
Ulcers malignant	Anemone
Varicose condition	Marigold, Carrot, Jack-by-the-hedge
Venereal Diseases	Marshmallow
Whooping cough	Chestnut, Coltsfoot, Garlic
Warts	Catmint, Dandelion
Worms	Aspen, Flax, Thyme
Wounds—internal	Burnet, Daisy
Wounds—external	Chickweed, Eryngo

herbs for healing

ADDERS TONGUE
Ophioglossum vulgatum. Once a popular herb but one which has been less used in more recent times. The juice can be employed to bathe several eye inflammations, and the leaves may be gently placed over tender chilblains. This is a herb whose leaves can be applied to wounds.

The juice and the leaves are used.

AGRIMONY
Agrimonia eupatoria. (See illustration on page 17). This grows widely in the temperate zones and is found in hedgerows, ditches, fields, heaths and woods. It is a great help for skin troubles; it can be used for the relief of asthma, bronchial troubles, jaundice and rheumatism.

Combined with equal parts of Raspberry leaf it will arrest diarrhoea. Many herbalists have used Agrimony successfully for liver disorders of all kinds.

Leaves and flowers used.

ALDER
Alnus glutinosa. This tree is easily identifiable. A decoction of leaves is good for placing on burns. It was often used to alleviate dropsy and gangrene by means of poultices made of moistened leaves and warm water—applied externally.

Leaves or powdered bark used.

ALL HEAL

Stachys sylvatica. (See illustration on page 17).
This is a famous old herb used for wounds. The
herb was an ancient " first aid " plant; the leaves were
bruised and applied directly to a wound both to stop
bleeding and heal the hurt. Made into a decoction it
has been used for the relief of cramp and aches in
joints.

Leaves used.

ANEMONE

Anemone Nemorosa. The juice of this plant's
leaves was used to bathe lepers and to cleanse malignant
ulcers.

An ointment made of the leaves was applied to
the eyelids to relieve cataract and opaque corneas.

Leaves used.

ARCHANGEL

Archangelica umbelliferae. The juice of its leaves
has long been used as an effective eye tonic. Decoctions
made from this plant can help heartburn, indigestion,
and will relieve coughs—it facilitates expectoration in
cases of pleurisy and is most useful in eliminating
waste products through the urine.

Leaves, flowers and seeds are used.

ASPARAGUS

Asparagus officinalis. This is, of course, the familiar vegetable you can purchase in the shops or grow in
your own garden. Do not despise the leaves (or
" fern "). The shoots are especially valuable for cor-
recting irregularity of the lymphatic system, and to
relieve dropsy, jaundice and unnaturally rapid action of

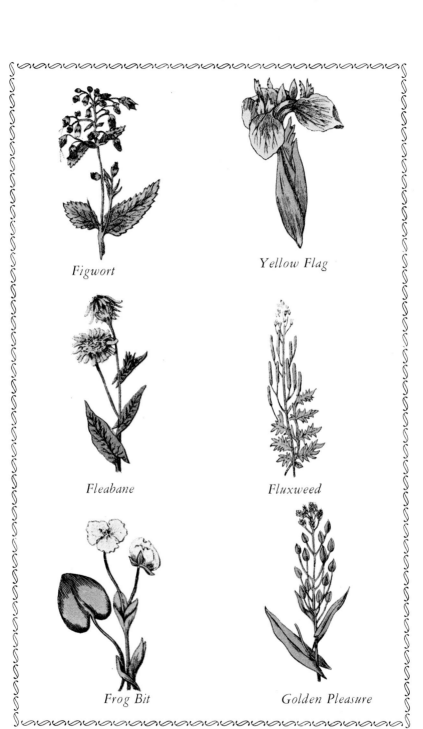

Figwort

Yellow Flag

Fleabane

Fluxweed

Frog Bit

Golden Pleasure

Goutwort

Harts Tongue

Houndstongue

Black Hoarhound

White Hoarhound

Haresfoot

the heart. It has long been esteemed for its action on all obstructions in bladder, gall and kidneys. It can be eaten raw, cooked, or made into a decoction.

Shoots and fern used.

ASPEN

Populus tremula. The powdered bark of twigs provides a medicine for the relief of feverous conditions (it contains Populin and Salicin). It is a fairly strong antidote for worms. Two heaped teaspoonfuls of the powder to one pint of boiling water. When cool drink one egg-cupful three times daily.

The bark is used.

AVENS

Geum urbanum. Older herbals have claimed a large number of healing properties for this plant. The powdered root might be employed as a substitute for quinine and as such can alleviate serious feverish conditions, dysentery, etc. It has fairly powerful antiseptic properties and is rather astringent.

One old authority recommends it for the condition we now refer to as leucorrhoea.

The powdered root is used.

BALM

Melissa officinalis. This pleasant scented plant grows in many woodlands and gardens, and its lemon-like smell is very attractive. It hinders senility, and is said to remedy impotence, to expel the placenta (after-birth) and to heal poisoned bites or stings. I first learnt of its uses when at Heidelberg University, in Germany tea made of *Melissa* is very popular. It encourages sweating, and is extremely beneficial for nervous dis-

orders; it relieves fevers and eases the pains of dysentery. Once herbalists would use the juice of this plant mixed with salt to remove wens or hard swellings on the flesh or in the throat.

The leaves or flowers can be used.

BARLEY

Hordeum pratense. This can be bought at any herbal shop. It has long been considered one of the most sound nerve tonics known. Cook lightly.

The grain is used.

BEANS

Faba. There are several varieties, and apart from eating them cooked as vegetables we can get a flour made of beans and use it for the relief of swollen testicles (making a poultice with a little wine and olive oil); it was also frequently applied to swellings on the breasts, and to the eyelids where there was excessive watering of the eyes.

Bean flour is used.

BEDSTRAW

Galium verum. (See illustration on page 17). This is also widely known as Ladies' Bedstraw. Although this has long been recommended for the relief of epileptics, there is not a great deal of information as to which types of epilepsy were relieved by it. Hysteria and many other nervous conditions were also treated with this herb.

The herb is used.

BEECH

Fagus sylvatica. This lovely tree, often called the

56

" Queen of the Forest " has the reputation of being the only tree that is never struck by lightning. Its leaves used to be made into a decoction to relieve diabetes. Certainly the decoction may be used to wash skin which is diseased.

The leaves are used.

BERGAMOT

Monarda Fistulosa. Relaxing for the nerves and for a nervy stomach.

The leaves are used.

BETONY

Betonica officinalis. (See illustration on page 18). Sufferers from rheumatic ailments will find that a tea made of Wood Betony and the juice of half a lemon (or orange) is warming, strengthening and brings considerable relief from the aches and pains of their illness. It also cleanses the bladder and kidneys well.

The leaves are used.

BILBERRY

Vaccinium myrtillus. Not only can we eat the berries fresh or make jam from them but we can use the leaves to make a decoction against all forms of catarrh, colds and throat ailments.

The leaves and berries are used.

BIRCH

Betula pendula. I have lived with Finns a lot, and from one of them I learnt that the leaves of the lovely Silver Birch could be used to make a decoction against rheumatic ills, catarrh, gout, dropsy and to relieve

57

stones in the bladder or kidney. The plant is extremely strong and a powerful diuretic, not more than seven leaves should be used to one and a half pints of boiling water, and when it has fully infused (like tea does) you can drink a teacupful twice a day.

The leaves are used.

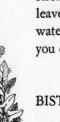

BISTORT

Polygonum bistorta. (See illustration on page 18). An extremely simple herb to identify and once a greatly favoured remedy for the treatment of diabetes although I do not personally have any record as yet of its success in the treatment of the ailment. It is an astringent with some mineral salts in its constitution, and is most commonly used to make a wholesome mouthwash and gargle, and it takes a lot of ingenuity to find a better.

The leaves or the powdered root are used.

BLACKBERRY

Rubus fruticosus. Apart from the nutritious berries you can make a decoction from the leaves and use it to relieve anaemia and to stop diarrhoea.

The leaves and berries are used.

BLACKCURRANT

Ribes nigrum. The berries are a rich source of Vitamin C, they and the leaves can be made into a decoction to relieve catarrh, colds, coughs and sore throats.

The leaves and berries are used.

BONESET

Eupatorium perfoliatum. This is a herb with a

history that goes back nearly three thousand years. The crushed leaves applied externally to a broken or fractured bone have long been esteemed efficacious in speeding the mending of the bone. It is known that the human body can absorb the chemical constituents of many substances through the skin.

There is no harm in using this in a decoction as described, and drinking two egg-cupfuls after breakfast and two more after supper.

The leaves or flowers are used.

BROOKLIME

Veronica becabunga. (See illustration on page 18). This is a herb which has very powerful diuretic properties and can be employed for all such conditions where the use of diuretics is considered judicious. It has a reputation as an antiscorbutic herb.

The leaves are used.

BROOM

Spartium scoparium. A very familiar plant of the heathlands. A powerful purgative, it also greatly increases the flow of urine. Three teaspoonfuls of Broom tops (collect only the top inch off of any shoot) to one pint of boiling water. It has long been recommended by herbalists for dropsy, gallstone, and liver complaints.

The tops of the shoots only are used.

BUCKBEAN

Meyanthus trifoliata. (See illustration on page 18). For all the people who suffer from loose teeth, weak undernourished gums and similar oral complaints the leaves of this plant will be a real boon. The

59

mixture should not be made too strong for this is a powerful purgative.

The leaves of Buckbean can be taken fresh and applied to all sorts of swollen glands, and some authorities claim that it will relieve mumps. Some success has been recorded in the use of this plant for dropsy. There is a warning which I must extend about this plant. The tea or decoction made of the leaves is almost tasteless, and there is a considerable danger that this will incline the user to think that it is not effective and so to increase the quantity of herb. It has very powerful purgative effects if this is done and should be kept to the proportion of half an ounce of dried leaves to one pint of boiling water.

The leaves are used.

BURNET

Sanguisorba minor

or S. officinalis. (See illustration on page 18). A herb long recommended for internal bleeding and deep internal wounds. It is considered as quite harmless and safe to use. Normal decoction, half a tea-cupful twice or thrice a day.

The leaves are used.

BURNET SAXIFRAGE

Pimpinella saxifraga. (See illustration on page 18). This attractive plant was once commonly used for relieving indigestion, and might be tried by those who do not like the taste of parsley for this purpose.

The leaves are used.

BUTCHERS BROOM

Ruscus aculeatus. (See illustration on page 17).
I have no experience of using this herb, but it is
interesting that older herbalists used the berries to make
a medicine which they claimed healed gonorrhoea, certainly this should be researched.

The berries were used.

CALAMINT

*Thymum calaminta. (See illustration on page
17).* There are many conditions of the muscles, and
particularly of the leg muscles which produce sensations
of cramp, pains and aches etc., which are very uncom-
fortable for the sufferer. Fresh leaves of Calamint will
relieve many such aches.

The leaves are used.

CAMOMILE

Anthemis nobilis. (See illustration on page 17).
Care must be taken if collecting this herb, others look
quite similar. Useful for female complaints, hysteria,
sleeplessness and nervous illnesses.

The leaves and flowers are used.

CARROT

Daucus carota. The root and the seed are used for
their great tonic properties, they are rich in minerals
and vitamins. Carrot juice is good for ailments of the
eyes, varicose conditions, hard swellings and diabetes.
Many kidney complaints have been helped by raw
carrot or the juice, and some herbalists claimed carrot
juice as a great help in early stages of cancer. The juice
must be extracted from raw carrots.

Root and seed are used.

CARROT (WILD)

Daucus sylvestris. (See illustration on page 17). The leaves of the Wild Carrot were often the handiest to grab hold of by a wounded man, and it has been handed down through the ages that they are effective to apply to cuts, sores and wounds, and made even more so if a thin layer of pure honey is placed over them.

The leaves are used.

CATMINT

Nepeta cataria. (See illustration on page 35). A tonic tea can be made from the leaves of this plant, and the fresh leaves can be applied directly to the anus to relieve haemorrhoids.

The leaves are used.

CELANDINE

Chelidonium majus. (See illustration on page 35). The juice of the plant dissolves warts, and can also be applied to circles of ringworms. An ointment made of the juice of the leaves and pure fat (*e.g.* coconut fat) can be applied to piles. *This is a herb best kept for external use by the layman.*

The leaves are used.

CELERY

Apium graveolens. The seeds dissolve many of the harmful accretions of uric acid; a decoction made of the seeds is a great help in rheumatic illnesses, it is diuretic and a tonic. The drink may be used with much success in arthritis, and cases of high blood pressure.

The seeds are used.

CENTAURY

Erythroea centaurium. (See illustration on page 35). The herb has considerable value as a tonic, and as such may be taken as a tea, although like many tonics, it has a slightly bitter taste. It tones up the liver, eases difficult and painful menstruation, and often increases its flow. Centaury has some effect as a febrifuge.

The leaves are used.

CHERRY

Cerasus duracina or *Juliana* etc. The water from a pan of boiled cherries contains considerable nutriment and some healing properties. It is recommended for indigestion, for dissolving gravel in the bladder and kidneys by many authors. It is well known that soothing relief can be gained by administering a mixture of cherry juice and honey to all cases of coughs and bronchitis, it soothes especially pharyngitis and laryngitis.

The fruit is used.

CHERVIL

Anthriscus cerefoliata or *Chaerophyllum aromaticum.* Decoctions made from the leaves make a most stimulating tonic. Making the decoction with whey instead of water has been a century old remedy for asthma. The famous herbalist Culpeper used it to cure pleurisy.

The leaves are used.

CHESTNUT

Castanea vulgaris. This is NOT the Horse Chestnut tree but the edible Chestnut. Whooping Cough or any convulsive cough can be powerfully relieved by a mixture of dried, powdered nuts and honey.

The nuts are used.

CHESTNUT/HORSE C.

Aesculus hippocastanum. In spite of its name in the English language this familiar tree is not related too closely to the ordinary edible chestnut tree. From the powdered nuts a specific against piles, rectal infection, pruritis and rectal pains can be made, applied externally.

The nuts are used.

CHICKWEED

Stellaria media. (See illustration on page 36). This humble herb contains some substances which I can best describe as unclassified vitamins; it is known now to be rich in mineral salts. It can be consumed raw as a salad. For wounds and ulcers one can apply the freshly washed herb straight to the place, the whole is then covered with a clean bandage, then renewed at equal intervals four times daily, using fresh herb. The fresh herb can also be applied safely to skin eruptions, styes; some old authorities used it for erysipelas. Mixed in equal parts with Elecampane *(Inula Viscosa)* it was recommended as a remedy for hydrophobia, by decoction internally.

The whole herb is used.

CINQUEFOIL

Potentilla-rosaceae. Many varieties. This is a herb with a most honourable history in the art of healing. A decoction can be used for gargles and mouth washes, as a fine skin lotion. It had a good reputation for stopping nose-bleeding and stopping excessive menstruation. Before the advent of quinine the powdered root was taken in a glass of wine to relieve malaria—for which it was considered very effective. The juice pressed from the roots relieves ulcerated kidneys and jaundice. The two commonest varieties are the *Potentilla canadensis* and the *Potentilla pamilla*.

The roots and the leaves are used.

CLARY

Salvia sclarea or *Salvia horminum*. Either of these varieties can be used. The seeds are placed at the corner of the eyes where within a very short time they become coated with mucus and impurities, they are so big as to slide out of the eye very easily, cleansing the eye as they go. They would appear to have been used for cases of cataract.

The seeds are used.

CLOVER (RED)

Trifolium pratense. This is a powerful cleanser of the blood, and a herb which has a long record of successful treatment of cancer. The washed flowers may be eaten raw, or one may make a decoction from dried flowers, or a wine. The White Clover is by no means so powerful and no substitute.

The flowers are used.

COLT'S FOOT

Tussilago farfara. (See illustration on page 36). Asthma, bronchitis, coughs, pleurisy, pneumonia, tuberculosis and whooping cough have all been cured with Colt's Foot. It is most useful to aid expectoration. It is a very frequent constituent in herbal tobaccos (so

65

that they are very safe to smoke). You need three tea-spoonfuls of the dried herb to one pint of boiling water to make a good decoction; it is slightly bitter to taste.

The leaves are used.

COLUMBINES

Aquelegia vulgaris. Decoctions of this plant are most helpful for opening obstructions in the liver and clearing up jaundice. It also makes a useful gargle.

The leaves are used.

COMFREY

Symphytum officinalis. (See illustration on page 17). This is one of the most unique and valuable herbs known to Botanic Medicine. The old country-man's name " knitbone " infers what the herb can do. Over any fracture or broken bone place a poultice of the leaves (dry or fresh), preferably the leaves should be chewed by the patient and, mixed with his own spittle, placed directly onto the place (this may sound primitive but it *is* extremely effective, I have tried it myself). The whole is lightly bandaged and left for 24 hours, then a fresh dressing is applied. This herb is also recommended for hernia, duodenal and gastric ulcers, and tuberculosis—all of which illnesses are found wherever there is a marked lack of Silica in the diet. Comfrey is one of the richest sources of this mineral salt in the botanic world, equalled only by Horsetail Grass *(Equisetum arvense)*. A decoction is made and drunk concurrently with the external appli-cations.

The leaves are used.

CORN MARIGOLD

Chrysanthemum segetum. (See illustration on page 35). In spite of its name in English this is not a true marigold but one of the humbler relatives of the Chrysanthemum family.

I cannot comment on the reputation it has for healing smallpox, as is claimed for it by older herbalists. But it is on record as being effective in relieving measles, jaundice and some other illnesses. The fresh juice is noted as a specific against warts.

The leaves are used, or the juice.

COWSLIP

Primula veris. This lovely spring ornament of field and woodside has many virtues, among which are the removal of freckles and skin blemishes by external application. A decoction drunk was held to allay epileptical attacks, St. Vitus Dance and many similar nervous and hysterical manifestations. It is a mild, tranquillizing herb, helpful for insomnia.

The flowers are used.

CRANESBILL

Geranium molle. (See illustration on page 35). A decoction can be made of the leaves of this herb and applied as a lotion to aching muscles, joints, and to several rheumatic conditions. It is for external use.

The leaves are used.

CROSSWORT

Valentia cruciata. (See illustration on page 36). This is one of those herbs which has tended to become a little neglected during the ages.

One of the areas for which it was considered most

effective was in the healing of hernias. To relieve a hernia and strengthen the muscle fibres a few leaves of Crosswort were placed against the skin and an appropriate truss applied over the area. The leaves have to be renewed daily. Also, a tea of the herb can be made and drunk by the patient.

Hernia patients should avoid constipation, keep free from coughs and all physical strain in the area affected by their rupture.

A good diet with plenty of silica foods and regular exercise under supervision has restored many a rupture to a painless condition, and many can be reduced completely.

The leaves are used.

CUDWEED

Gnaphalium vulgare. (See illustration on page 17). A decoction is made at the strength of one ounce to one pint of boiling water.

When it is cool the lotion can be painted on over mumps and several conditions of swollen glands, and then some of the decoction weakened with water by 50% can be drunk as a cold tea.

The leaves are used.

DAFFODILS

Narcissus pseudonarcissus. The roots may be cut open and applied to bad sprains and strains, or to aching joints.

The roots are used.

DAISY (OXEYE)

Bellis perennis. A tea can be made from the simple leaves of this well-loved plant, so often a favourite

68

with children. Its medical uses are considerable, but it is principally recommended for relief of internal inflammations and wounds, and externally as a most useful antiseptic lotion to bathe cuts, sores, ulcers and wounds. It is also safe for bathing the genitalia.

The leaves are used.

DANDELION

Taraxacum officinalis. Was formerly described as *Leontodon taraxacum.* This familiar plant is a most valuable herbal medicine. The juice of the fresh plant can be applied directly to warts, corns and hard dermatic swellings. A decoction made of the leaves or the flowers can be used to cleanse the blood, to ease diabetes, obesity, to increase the flow of urine (which we must remember carries away the waste and debris of our bodies), it has been shown to be of use in many types of lymphatic illnesses; it is a gentle laxative and cases of dropsy have yielded to a prolonged treatment with Dandelion. A coffee substitute is made from the ground roots, it is pleasant tasting and free from caffeine.

The leaves and flowers are chiefly used.

DARNEL (RED)

Lolium rubrum. (See illustration on page 36). A poultice of the leaves may be employed to aid the extraction of splinters or embedded stones or dirt in a wound. It also removes bone splinters in the same way.

The leaves are used.

DEVIL'S BIT

Scabiosa succisa. (See illustration on page 36).

The juice or leaves are used to make a wholesome wash to clear up the skin from pimples, eruptions, even from freckles.

DOCK (RED)
Rumex aquaticus. When I was a child I was taught to put dock leaves over stings or bites and when stung by stinging nettles. A decoction of fresh leaves cools down overheated blood. The juice of the roots boiled in vinegar applied externally to sores, leprous (and even venereal) was considered to be a powerful specific.

The leaves or the roots are used.

DODDER OF THYME
Cusculata europaea. A herb has been used for relieving kidney complaints and some ailments of the bladder.

The leaves are used.

DROPWORT
Oenanthc fistulosa. (See illustration on page 36). The root was sometimes used to relieve a stoppage in the bladder. It acts as an expectorant, and makes a good gargle.

The root was used.

EARTHNUT
Conopodium majus. (See illustration on page 36). Once a popular treat for country children who would dig up the nuts and roast them just as they still do chestnuts. There seems to be a nutritious quality, and some mineral salts in them.

70

Jacinth   Liverwort   Juniper Shrub

Jack-by-the-Hedge   Knapweed   Motherwort

Meadowsweet   Mullein   Mustard

Marshmallow

Pellitory of the Wall

Soapwort

Scurvy Grass

Tansy

Violet

ELDER

Sambucus nigra. The Father of Medicine, Hippocrates, was one of the first herbalists to praise the many uses of this familiar and valuable plant. A decoction of the leaves will help eczemous conditions (applied externally and drunk as well), it is a pleasant and gentle laxative. The flowers (dried) can be used to make a powerful decoction to drink against colds, for healthy complexion and as a mixture to give a lovely sheen to the hair. The decoction of the flowers can also be used in your eye bath as a valuable eye-lotion.

The berries make a most nutritious drink for colds, coughs, they ease difficult menstruation, and help sore throats.

The leaves, flowers, and berries are used.

ELECAMPANE

Inula viscosa. Place two teaspoonfuls of the dried leaves in a basin, pour on some boiling water; lean your head over it, cover head and basin with a towel so that you inhale the herb-perfumed steam. This will greatly help asthma, hayfever, sinus conditions, and any feelings of having blocked sinus, blocked nose or throat. It is not an unpleasant smell. A decoction of the leaves used as a mouthwash regularly is said to strengthen the gums; drunk the same will rid the body of worms. It is held that decoctions made from the washed root are stronger than those of the leaves of the herb.

The leaves and sometimes the root used.

ERYNGO

Eryngium campestre. (See illustration on page 36). The boiled roots were applied to a wound with badly torn flesh, and are on record as speeding up the natural growth processes.

The roots were used.

EYEBRIGHT

Euphrasia officinalis. (See illustration on page 36). The power of this herb in healing diseases of the eye has never been questioned. The juice squeezed regularly into the eyes has occasionally restored sight to the blind, it strengthens the sight.

The juice is used.

FENNEL

Foeniculum officinale. One of the oldest, safest and most trustworthy of medicinal herbs. It has long been used to help fat people reduce their girth and weight. In my book " Herbal Teas for Health and Pleasure " I mentioned what a popular tea this can make. All stomach and gastric disorders can benefit from the use of Fennel: Cramp in the muscles, many forms of rheumatic and arthritic ills can be relieved by the regular use of Fennel Tea. Delayed or painful menstruation is often treated by herbalists by decoctions of Fennel seed. Some herbalists recommend the foliage (particularly against nervous strain) but I personally have always used the seeds. Some cases in which diabetics have responded to treatment by this herb are on record.

The seeds are used.

FENUGREEK

Trigonella-Foenum graecum. Commonly used for increasing the flow of milk in mothers; pregnant women have used this herb for many centuries to strengthen themselves and ease labour. A poultice of

74

the crushed seeds made either with a warm liquid (milk or water) or in emergency with human spittle can be applied to abscesses, carbuncles, etc., cover the whole wth a clean adhesive plaster or bandage.

The seeds are used.

FEVERFEW

Chrysanthemum parthenium. A tea can be made from the leaves which can help most of the commoner female complaints. It is a tonic.

FIGWORT

Scrophularis nodosa. (See illustration on page 53). Apply freshly crushed leaves to contusions and all similar bad bruisings. The juice has properties which brings out the bruise and facilitates the healing processes.

The leaves are used.

FLAG (YELLOW)

Iris luteus. (See illustration on page 53). The juice of the plant is considered helpful to relieve many eye ailments.

FLAX

Linum usitatissimum. Some herbalists use this for many remedies, but I can best recommend it for inflammation of the intestines and to cure worms. Use in a decoction.

The seed is used.

FLEABANE

Erigeron canadensis. (See illustration on page 53). There are various forms of this herb but the

75

Canadensis has increased in popularity over the last century particularly because of its reputation for relieving severe fevers *e. g.* Typhus. Incidentally our forebears named the plant well, fleas seem terrified of it. Use internally as a decoction or externally as a wash to keep off fleas, etc.

The leaves, flowers or seeds are used.

FLUXWEED

Sisymbrium sophia (See illustration on page 53). For use against diarrhoea and as an anthelmintic. Once used as a poultice to speed up the healing of broken bones.

The whole herb was used.

FROG BIT

Hydrocaris morcus ranae. (See illustration on page 53). This plant is a kind of water-lily. The leaves are applied externally. Bruise the leaves and apply to sores, swellings that are hot and painful.

The leaves are used.

FUMITORY

Fumaria officinalis. Biliousness, all liver complaints, sickness and exhaustion from digestive disorders are helped by this simple wayside plant.

The flowers and leaves are used.

GARLIC

Allium sativum. This strong-smelling medicine is not a native of English fields but can be cultivated. It was one of the most successful remedies against the Great Plague. Virgil and Pliny both wrote in praise of its medicinal virtues. It is probably one of the most powerful antiseptics known to Man: Catarrh simply cannot persist against Garlic. Its oil penetrates to almost every single tissue of the body, and can actually be traced in the perspiration within hours after eating just one or two cloves. All kinds of worms are destroyed by Garlic. Many inmates of concentration camps owe their health and survival to regular doses of Garlic. Arthritis, Asthma, Blood Pressure, Fevers (including Typhoid), Pleurisy, Tuberculosis, Whooping Cough, and many other serious diseases have been treated with Garlic by herbalists down the ages. I have used this herb frequently myself and obtained excellent results in a variety of cases. It is a speedy help in cases of pharyngitis and laryngitis.

I must admit that the smell is somewhat overpowering, and the taste is one best gotten over quickly. Some patients have foolishly refused Garlic on account of its smell and taste, but anybody who exhibits such behaviour is more in need of a psychologist than any other form of healer. The dose varies from one to three cloves of Garlic eaten raw, and preferably chewed slowly. Some shops sell Garlic Perles (capsules containing the oil) which can be swallowed without tasting or smelling it.

The cloves are used.

GENTIAN

Gentiana lutea (yellow)

or *Gentiana campestris* (blue). Herbalists have always tended to recommend this as a remedy against poisonous bites, from snakes, dogs, animals or insects. Take as a decoction internally, and apply a powder of the root to the wound. The decoction will need a sweetening agent (molasses, honey, brown sugar, etc.) for it is not a popular taste. As bites may involve secondary infections, tetanus or other conditions the patient is advised to seek expert advice at the earliest opportunity —particularly after snake bite, or animal bites.

The root is used, mostly powdered.

GINGER

Zingiber officinale. This makes a cheering tonic and a mild stimulant, particularly when one is suffering from depression. As decoction, tea or wine.

The powdered root is used.

GINSENG

Panax quinquefolium. Only available by importation from the Far East. The wonder herb of China, used for five millennia to cure all manner of diseases and to ward off old age. Decoction.

The powdered root is used.

GLADWIN (SMELLY)

Iris foetidissima. The juice can be placed over thorns or foreign bodies in the flesh and will aid their removal.

The leaves are used.

GOLDEN ROD

Solidage odora or *S. virgaurea.* In my travels through Central Europe and the Balkans I have been amazed to learn how popular the tea made from this plant is. An uncle who was a trapper in Northern Canada reported that the Indians formerly used it as a tonic drink. For any digestive troubles, kidney complaint, or just a tonic it is a great help. In olden days it was widely employed against tuberculosis.

The leaves are used.

GOLDEN PLEASURE

Camelina sativa. (See illustration on page 53).
A poultice can be made for any severe inflammation.
The flowers and topmost leaves are used.

GOLDEN SEAL

Hydrastis canarensis. This is the plant called
Turmeric by grocers, from its oriental name. Eczema,
Erysipelas, Eye disorders or infections of the genital
organs have all been treated with Golden Seal. It can
be eaten raw, with a little milk and brown sugar, or
made into a decoction.
The powdered root is used.

GROUNDSEL

Senecio vulgaris. This makes a fine remedy against
chapped hands by making a poultice from seeds or
leaves. It is a popular bird-food.
The leaves and seeds are used.

GOUTWORT

Podagraria. (See illustration on page 54). The
juice or the decoction of the leaves can be applied
gently to gouty limbs and brings relief.

HARESFOOT

Pes leporinus. (See illustration on page 54).
Country people used to take a few leaves of this plant
and place them in their socks to prevent heavy perspiration of the feet. It is very relaxing to use them in
this way if you have a long walk before you.

HARTS TONGUE

Scolopendrium vulgaris. (See illustration on page

54). If none of the usual liver tonics are available recourse might be made to this plant which once had a great reputation for cleansing and healing the liver.
The leaves are used.

HAWTHORN

Crataegus monogyna. This pleasantly flowering shrub is a most useful source of healing properties.

From the dried leaf comes relief from all cardiac ills, asthma, dropsy, and many ailments ranging from a sore throat to the breaking up of cholesterol deposits in the arteries. A tea or decoction is made.
The leaves are used.

HEARTSEASE

Viola tricolor. This has always been respected for the help that it can bring to epileptics, and any convulsive sickness. It is the Wild Pansy.
The leaves are used.

HEATHER

Any member of the *Ericaceae* family.

From this beautiful and aromatic plant you can make a decoction to use against coughs, colds, the run down feeling, general depression, and a really remarkable list of nervous ills and conditions which border on the psycho-somatic field of medicine. It helps those who cannot sleep to rest—particularly if administered with honey and warm milk.
The leaves and buds are used.

HOARHOUND

Marrubium vulgare or *M. nigrum. (See illustration on page 54).* This herb can be used to make a splendid gargle or an expectorant. It will often help a sore throat when all else has failed. Taken inwardly as a decoction it is a fine stimulating tonic, but should not be taken in large quantities otherwise it will prove to be a very effective laxative.

The leaves and flowers are used.

HOLLYHOCK

Althea Rosa. Since olden days this was administered to prevent miscarriage, and to heal diseases of the womb, vagina and female troubles generally. In Germany it is a longstanding remedy for weak heart action and all cardiac troubles.

The flowers are used (dried).

HONEYWORT

Cerinthe majus. The juice of the plant was used widely for eye diseases, but the exact description of these has not been clearly indicated.

HOPS

Humulus lupulus. The sedative effects of hops have been known for thousands of years; they alleviate pain, induce sleep, lessen abnormal sexual desire, and remove restlessness from sleeping patients. Sometimes people used to fill a pillow with hops to induce sleep. Anaemia can be helped by decoction of hops drunk regularly. It must be stressed that hops in decoction are slightly different in their effects to hops made into beer. A fomentation made of hops was recommended by more than one herbalist for the treatment externally of hard swellings and tumours. There are some interesting traces of mineral salts in hops.

The fruit and the leaves are used.

HORSETAIL GRASS

Equisetum arvense. One of the richest sources of Silica. A most useful herb if you have brittle finger nails, undernourished skin, epistaxis (nose bleeding), or earache. Practically no herb looks so like its own name as does this, it really resembles a horses tail held upside down. A continental colleague assures me that it makes an excellent eye-wash, especially for the older person. *Half ounce to a pint.*

The whole herb is used.

HOUNDSTONGUE

Cynoglossum vulgaris. (See illustration on page 54). The juice of the leaves was used to stop falling hair. The leaves were bruised and applied directly to haemorrhoids.

The juice or the leaves are used.

ICELANDIC MOSS

Cetraria islandica. Despite its name this herb is found widely in Britain as well as in all northern countries. In Lapland the reindeer can live on it and to see these powerful animals one realizes that the herb has exceptionally valuable nutritional properties. It has a slightly bitter taste which humans do not enjoy as much as reindeer! Certainly cases of rickets have been helped by including this plant in the patient's diet. I was once engaged to a lovely Icelandic girl who told me that the country-folk of her land used this plant to heal tuberculosis of the lungs. Those senior citizens who feel frail will benefit by using Icelandic Moss.

This herb must be prepared as follows:—

Three teaspoonfuls of the plant (heaped up) to one pint of water; place in an enamel saucepan and simmer gently until you can see a jelly-like substance forming. *DO NOT BOIL!* Drink when cool, a teacupful at a time.

The whole plant is used.

IRISH MOSS

Chondrus crispus. This is also nourishing. It is especially beneficial for bladder and kidney complaints. Much success has also been claimed for it in case of respiratory diseases. Prepare in the same way as Icelandic Moss.

The whole plant is used

IVY

Hedera helix. Yes, this much abused and hated parasite has also medical virtues, which our forefathers knew and used widely. It became neglected in the great economic debacle of the Industrial Revolution at the beginning of the 19th Century when so much herbal lore was lost.

Bruise the leaves and the berries and apply directly to any stiff or " rheumaticky " joints. The juice can be gently applied externally to glandular swellings, such as mumps.

THIS HERB IS FOR EXTERNAL USE ONLY.
The berries and leaves are used.

JACINTH

Hyacinthus nonscriptus. (See illustration on page 71). The juice has quite powerful styptic qualities.

JACK-BY-THE-HEDGE

Sisymbrium alliara. (See illustration on page 71).
The juice or the decoction of the leaves can be
used to massage varicose conditions and ulcers. As a tea
it is said to aid bladder, kidney and similar conditions.
The leaves are used.

JUNIPER

*Juniperus communis. (See illustration on page
71).* The juice of the berries can be massaged
into joints where there is sciatica. It is unwise to take
this herb internally without the advice of a practitioner
of Botanic Medicine.

KNAPWEED

Centaurea scabiosa. (See illustration on page 71).
Either juice or leaves of this herb can be employed
to alleviate nose bleeding or other forms of external
bleeding. There is some relief for bruises too.

KUMMEL

Carum carui. This is the familiar household Caraway. And it is a very good drink to treat gallbladder
disease with. Many sufferers from colic and indigestion
have found relief in Caraway tea. One desertspoonful
seeds to 1 pint of water.
The seeds are used.

LAVENDER

Lavendula vera. There is another variety the
Lavendula spica, and either can be used to make a
decoction that is a potent easer of the pains of tooth-

ache, for relief of headaches, strengthening the gums when the teeth are loose, and calming down a nervous stomach.

The flowers and top shoots are used.

LEADWORT

Plumbago europaea. This humble denizen which often infests private smallholdings and gardens is not to be despised. It has some power to excite saliva, and to relieve the pains of toothache. It has a rather hot taste if chewed.

The plant has an extremely high acid content.

The leaves, flowers or root are used.

LEMON

Citrus limonum. The commonly used household lemon has so many virtues that a book might be compiled on it alone. In my many wanderings I have never failed to stop and look at lemon trees, they are so beautiful, the fruit hangs on them like precious jewels from a necklace.

There are over twenty varieties of lemon but the juice of all of them is most helpful as a remedy for purifying the blood, for bleaching the skin, for rubbing into the scalp against falling hair, and for using mixed in any shampoo to act as a tonic to the scalp. In the mountain villages of Serbia the peel of the lemon is kept in lavatories to act as a disinfectant and maintain the closet fresh (it is renewed every other day or so with fresh lemonpeel), so when you have squeezed all the juice out of your lemons, keep the skin either whole or in slices to put in your kitchen-bins or dustbins, etc.

From mediaeval times onwards the skin of a

85

lemon has been chewed to act as cleaner of teeth and a strengthening agent for the gums (spit it out afterwards).

If you have nothing else handy you can always apply fresh lemon juice to any cut or wound.

Naturopaths frequently recommend a course of lemon juice and water to rid the body of accumulated poisons and debris.

You can extract more juice from a lemon if you place it in an oven *for a few minutes* and bake it slowly. The humble lemon contains vitamins A, B, C, G, and the rare Vit. P. (which is in the white pithy part of the peel).

Dilute the juice and you can apply it (1 part of juice to 3 parts of water) to erysipelas, carbuncles, abcesses.

Dysentery quickly clears up after a few drinks of pure lemon juice. Some authorities in Botanic Medicine have used it quite successfully in the relief of diabetes.

Yellow jaundice and clotting of the arteries by cholesterol are alleviated by prolonged course of drinking lemon juice. Many diseases of the respiratory system can be helped by including lemon juice in the diet.

Generally speaking if you can stand the acidity you should drink the lemon juice raw, if you cannot then drink the juice of one lemon in a cup of cold or lukewarm water—never use hot water it destroys some of the Vitamin C content and this vitamin is particularly sensitive to heat. If you must have it sweetened the only sweetening agent allowable is pure honey.

The fruit is used.

LIQUORICE

Glycyrrhiza glabra. Not a native of Britain but easily imported from Spain or other Southern countries this familiar constituent of many childhood sweets has distinctive medical properties. The root is a powerful help in all cases of respiratory diseases, from the common cold up to pneumonia, pleurisy and even tuberculosis. It is popularly used as a perfectly safe laxative that even the smallest children can benefit by, and which calms down the stomach while consumed.

Once this herb was recommended to women who were barren because there seems to be ground for believing that liquorice can remedy this condition.

The root is used.

LIVERWORT

Lichens. (See illustration on page 71). This is, of course, an entire family of plants, and the reference in old herbals to Liverworts is a little frustrating, there are hundreds to choose from. Most of them are useful in alleviating ringworm, and some external skin infections.

LUCERNE

Medicago sattiva. This is found in Britain although a native of the Mediterranean countries, and America it is commonly called *Alfafa.* It is a plant which will put flesh on those who are undersized, it is extremely rich in minerals and in vitamins it cleanses the kidneys and may be taken safely by sufferers from arthritic and rheumatic diseases.

The leaves are used.

MARIGOLD

Calendula officinalis. From personal experience I recommend this herb most sincerely. There are few plants in the world which are so effective in clearing skin infections, eczema, erysipelas, warts, and much similar can all be cleared by a course of drinking a decoction of marigold flowers over a few days. In my teens I recovered from erysipelas on the cheek by this treatment.

It is fairly certain that some property in marigolds can keep the blood vessels young and healthy, prevent premature ageing and ward off senility.

A mixture of marigold flowers and witch-hazel will hasten the cure of any sprained muscles, and relieve conditions of muscular exhaustion.

Varicose conditions can be greatly alleviated by marigolds which could be taken frequently as a tea (see my work on " Herbal Teas ").

This is a very pleasant tonic drink, and it will ward off feverish conditions for those who are working among sick patients.

The flowers and the leaves are used.

MARJORAM

Origanum vulgare. All of the *Origanum* family seem to have beneficial actions for Mankind to use. In his *Indian Scout* (1864) Gustave Aimard refers to *Origanum Mexicana* as a herb for healing wounds, being applied with raw spirit mixed to the juice or the crushed leaves.

For our native variety, the Marjoram of English hills, I can recommend that it helps considerably to cure bad breath, to rid the patient of indigestion, to relieve the sickness in early stages of pregnancy and

88

alleviates nervous headaches or hangovers.
Flowers and leaves are used.

MARSHMALLOWS

Althaea officinalis. (See illustration on page 72).
A rather valuable herb whose flowers, leaves and
juice can be used. Herbalists have used this for
dermatic, respiratory, stomachic and venereal conditions. The familiar garden Hollyhock is also an
Althaea.
Flowers and leaves are used.

MEADOWSWEET

*Filipendula almaria. (See illustration on page
71).* The flowers are used for colic, dysentery and for
all types of stomachic conditions.

MEDLAR

Mespilus germanica. In our urban civilization not
everybody will be able to recognize a medlar tree when
they see one, so ask a countryman or use one of the
books recommended in the list included with this work.

Many herbalists used either a decoction of the un-
ripened fruit or else a poultice of the crushed fruit
applied externally in the region of the kidneys to prevent a miscarriage. Personally I have no experience of
this treatment, but it is worth noting.
The fruit is used.

MELLITOT

Melitotus officinalis. The long, spiked and strag-
gling flowers of this plant are the ornament of many a
hedgerow. The juice of the plant was used to remove

F   89 film (cataract) from the eye. Decoction of flowers relieves acidity.

The flowers or the juice are used.

MINT

Mentha viridis. This herb is the familiar Spearmint it can be relied upon to check vomiting. In many parts of the Islamic world the tradition has been handed down that this restores male fertility in men and in stallions.

The leaves are used.

N.B.   There are very many different varieties of the Mint family.

MOTHERWORT

Cardiaca leonurus. (See illustrations on page 71). The tops of the herb can be made into a tea which is rather helpful for most female complaints. It is a tonic for many cardiac conditions and can also be used in cases of hysteria.

The leaves are used.

MOUNTAIN HOLLY

Ilex aquilifolium. I was interested to read an American report that the juice of this plant's leaves had been applied to Tetanus and destroyed the infection. If there were no other help available at all it could be tried. In connection with Tetanus, however, I remember the extremely old country methods of dealing with it, and I mention them because sometimes such infections occur when there is no hospital to rush to. Method one was to expose the infection to the fumes of a slowly burning honeycomb. Method two, to apply a fresh poultice of milk to the wound every three hours (germs can multiply more easily in milk than in human flesh). Method three was to wash the wound and apply salt pork to the wound fairly tightly (on the same principle that germs would multiply more easily in the pork, and leave the flesh to do so). I haven't used these methods but I include them with the remark that success has been claimed for each of them.

MULLEIN

Verbascum album or *V. nigrum. (See illustration on page 71)*. A simple tea can be prepared which will be found effective against most colds and chest complaints. The juice can be applied to boils. Mixed in equal parts with Sage it can be used to bathe rheumatic limbs.

The leaves are used.

MUSTARD

Sinapis. (See illustration on page 71). Unless you have tried it you will scarcely credit the tremendous relief that can be gained by placing the feet in a bowl of hot water and mustard seed or powder. Impending colds, chills and rheumatic conditions can all be greatly alleviated and prevented if this simple, old-fashioned country remedy is employed as quickly as possible when the symptoms are noticed.

NETTLE

Urtica dioica. Go into any chemist, ask him how much it would cost you to buy some tablets containing Calcium, Chlorine, a trace of Copper, Potassium, Silicon, Sodium, together with traces of other minerals and vitamins. Before you pay the price asked go out along

a country lane, cut off the tops of the Stinging Nettle —and you have all of these in your hands for nothing! The plant was introduced as a first-class medicinal herb by the Romans, and now runs wild throughout the land. You can easily pick the plant with gloves on and your fingers then won't get stung. If you have a cut or wound you can apply clean nettle leaves straight on to it, they are rather effective in stopping bleeding. Anaemia, arthritis, dropsy, obesity, rheumatism, stone in the bladder or kidney, sciatica, sexual impotency and several other ailments will all be greatly relieved by use of Nettles.

The top leaves of the plants are used.

OATS

Avena sativa. This is called the " Black Oat " to distinguish it from a host of relatives. If you buy oat flakes you do not need to cook them further, you can eat them with warm (not hot) or cold milk. There is simply no other nerve tonic like them, they are naturally rich in vitamins and mineral salts. They can be used with perfect safety for a health-giving tonic. It is considered by several dieticians that the predominance of oats in the national diet of Scotland has contributed to the robust physique and equally robust nerves of the Scots. One dietician went so far as to attribute the height of the race (Scots are the tallest white race in the world) to the use of oats.

A dish of oatflakes, chopped fruit (two or three kinds) a handful of assorted nuts, and some cream or milk—brown sugar according to taste—and you have an astoundingly nourishing and healthy meal in one dish! There are innumerable variations you can make on this theme.

92

Oatflakes, chopped cheese, honey and warm milk also make a very nourishing dish.

The flakes or the grain are used.

ONION

Allium cepa. Many people do not realize that the onion has many medical properties, and it has the advantage of neither tasting as bitter nor smelling so highly as its cousin the garlic. Pliny listed no less than twenty-eight ailments that could be cured by onions. The juice of the onion is one of the most irresistible antiseptics and disinfectants in the world; experiments in Russia showed that typhus, streptococci, staphylococci and masses of other nasty, anti-social organisms yielded to onion-juice. Gangrene of wounds has been successfully treated by onion vapour (from freshly cut open onions) alone in Russia.

PARSLEY

Petroselinum sativum. Pregnant mothers should avoid this herb, either eating it raw or drinking it in decoction can facilitate a miscarriage.

Apply the raw leaves (slightly bruised) to any insect sting or bite for relief. Dirty wounds can be cleansed with Parsley leaves (they contain vitamins and mineral salts which are particularly good for the skin). Taken in decoction it makes a reliable tonic, but it tends to increase the flow of urine very heavily, in view of which it is often recommended to heal kidney disorders. Swollen glands are often treated with Parsley.

The leaves are used.

PELLITORY OF THE WALL

Parietaria officinalis. (See illustration on page 72). A tea can be made for the relief of coughs,

chills, sore throats etc., from the leaves. The leaves or the tea can be applied to cuts, sores, wounds and to cleanse ears from infection.

The leaves are employed.

PIMPERNEL

Anagallis arvensis. The juice is helpful for bee and wasp stings.

PINE

Pinus sylvestris. From the kernels of this graceful tree you can make a satisfactory decoction for alleviating lumbago. Use two average sized kernels to one pint of water.

The kernels are used.

POTATO

Solanum tuberosum. For once we have such a familiar plant that nobody needs cite the Latin name. The juice of a raw potato will really relieve many types of rheumatism and a crushed raw potato can be applied to a sore or wound, bandaged and left, change twice daily.

The housewife who burns herself in the kitchen will find quick relief if she applies a little raw potato juice (or inner side of peelings) to the burn.

The fruit of the plant is used.

RASPBERRY

Rubus idaeus. The leaves of this plant can be made into a pleasant decoction which lessens the chance of anaemia developing, and which renders childbirth easy. The traditional technique was to drink a cupful

94

once a day for between three and six months before labour was anticipated. It is said that this makes childbirth almost painless.

The leaves are used.

REST HARROW

Ononis arvensis. The powdered root is a powerful diuretic and has been found to be helpful in cases of extremely obstinate rheumatism.

The root is used.

ROSEHIPS

Rose canina. From these one can make a decoction and drink a little each day during the winter to help keep free from nasal and respiratory infections.

The hips contain seven vitamins and three mineral salts—so much for those men in the medical profession who, in all ignorance, used to sneer at herbal medicines! There is one word of caution, simmer this decoction, do not bring it to the boil or you will lose some of the Vitamin C content. Scandinavian Rosehips (due to soil conditions etc.) contain up to 6000Mg. of Vitamin C per 100 grams weight!

The ripe hips are used.

SAGE

Salvia officinalis or *Salvia agrestis.* A great tonic and a popular drink among some of the villages of Upper Macedonia (where it is called *Zhalfija*), and Greece partly because it is said to increase virility.

It is a good medium to allay fevers with, and many herbalists have used it for centuries to cure inflammations of the throat or of the uvula. Cramp in old people can be relieved by washing their limbs with decoction of Sage, the same treatment is held to be good for internal bruising.

It is a good herb to administer as a drink following shock or severe stress, emotional or intellectual. Applied to the hair it is restorative in some cases.

The leaves are used.

ST. JOHN'S WORT

Hypericum perforatum. This plant was once credited with the ability to heal numerous diseases, but I shall list only the most useful properties here. It can safely be put to any bites, bruises, burns, scalds, scratches etc., simply by crushing the leaves or whole top of the plant and bandaging it on.

The decoction is useful against dysentery, jaundice, liver ailments generally, internal ulcers and worms.

The flowers and top shoots of the plants used.

SCURVY GRASS

Cochlearia officinalis. (See illustration on page 72). The leaves make a most wholesome mouth wash which is very refreshing.

SEA-WRACK

Fucus vesiculosus. This is often called Bladderwrack, and is an easily identified form of brown seaweed.

I have known several cases of arthritic and rheumatic patients who have been positively cured by a regular course of Sea-wrack. It is certainly a powerful aid to stout people who wish to regain a smaller girth, and I rate it one of the best cures for such forms of obesity which have a rheumatic connection.

N.B. In this case use only three teaspoonfuls of the

dried and shredded plant to one pint of water. Its use greatly increases the flow of urine.

The dried plant is used.

SILVERWEED

Potentilla anserina. This is one of the commonest plants of the wayside. It acts as a strong astringent; makes a good gargle if you have a sore throat; can stay a heavy menstruation, reducing it to a more normal flow; and halts any diarrhoea. A tablespoonful of the dried, powdered herb was administered every four hours to bring down " ague " and fever.

The leaves are used.

SOAPWORT

Saponaria officinalis. (See illustration on page 72). If the leaves of this plant are used in warm water just as we agitate soap the effect will be exactly the same. They remove grease and dirt from hands and from clothes. Many skin ailments can be alleviated by external use of the leaves. For people who suffer from various allergies—especially to alkaline substances the use of soapwort is most helpful.

SPEEDWELL

Veronica officinalis. This pale blue flowered plant is a little gem in healing all sorts of eye troubles and has been known for this over many centuries. If the eyes are very weak indeed, make a decoction of the herb, three teaspoonfuls of dried herb to one pint of water and bathe the eyes at frequent intervals with it. Once or twice a day a piece of lint may be wrung out in this decoction and placed gently over the closed eyes of the patient. Do not expect miracles of it, but try it!

In most conditions the symptoms are so extremely varied that unless a remedy is tried, *nobody* could possibly say with 100% precision which remedy will produce best results.

Drunk, the same decoction is a good tonic for the blood.

The flowers and leaves are used.

SYCAMORE

Acer pseudoplatanus. From the bark of this very familiar tree we can make a powder which will act beneficially on open wounds, provides an astringent and has, according to some writers, a curative action in advance ophthalmia but of this last I have no experience. There can be no harm in trying. Cases have been recorded where herbs have restored sight to those who never expected to see again.

The bark is used.

TANSY

Tanacetum vulgare. (See illustration on page 72). A great favourite up to the time of grandparents at least, but now the popular " taste " is only for sweetened things. It comes very near to the attractive idea of being a panacea; some of the old herbalists had such a faith in it they used it for nearly every disease imaginable.

Certainly successes have been recorded in the use of Tansy for cases of dropsy, kidney and liver ailments, for all sorts of fevers, against palpitations of the heart and many cardiac conditions. The taste of Tansy is exceptionally strong but not really unpleasant; however, using three teaspoonfuls of herb to one pint of boiling water the dose should not exceed half a teacupful at a time. Boils, carbuncles and styes can be helped by the external application of the liquid described.

The flowers and leaves are used.

THYME

Thymus vulgaris. A good antiseptic for all throat, nasal and bronchial infections. *Thymol* means oil of Thyme. Good against colic and worms. A pleasant tonic drink. Sometimes a case of sinusitis will yield to a course of Thyme tea drinking. A tradition is that Hercules became a strong man through eating much Thyme with his meals.

The leaves, flowers and seeds used.

VERVAIN

Verbena officinalis. A great help in cases of nervous disorders of all kinds. Particularly renowned as an anti-convulsant, and as a cure for many eye conditions.

The flowers and leaves are used.

VIOLET

Viola odorata. (See illustration on page 72). Several cases have been recorded where the eating of fresh violet leaves over a long period has dissolved cancerous growths in the mouths and internally. All cancer patients should have themselves analysed; one of the world's leading cancer surgeons remarked that he had never known a single cancer patient without some deeply rooted mental problem. What we must always remember is that for thousands of years Man never knew of the existence of Vitamins or Mineral Salts, and it would be foolish to assume we know all

about them now; in some of these simple plants there are certainly hitherto unidentified healing substances which some future generations will be able to identify.

The flowers and leaves are used.

WALLFLOWERS

Cheiranthus cheiri. How often our gardens are ablaze with the lovely blooms of this familiar flower, and how few of us seem to know that the leaves can be used as a powerful tonic for the nerves and the muscles. Either as a decoction or chopped up as an extra " green " food on your dinner plate.

The leaves are used.

WATERCRESS

Nasturtium officinale. This familiar salad vegetable is extremely rich in mineral salts and vitamins.

It has long been considered a plant with which cancer may be healed, or alternatively if one eats of it regularly as a preventative of cancer. Cysts can be reduced by regular inclusion of Watercress in the diet. Eye conditions, rickets, fibrositis, lumbago, many rheumatic and similar conditions will be greatly alleviated by regular consumption of this plant.

The leaves and stalks are eaten fresh.

WATERLILY

Nymphoea alba. The decoction of the flowers makes a skin lotion with good cleansing properties. Once used as a beauty preparation.

WITCH-HAZEL

Hamamelis virginica. Most chemists sell extract of Witch-Hazel and it is a reliable antiseptic and

100

astringent with which to treat cuts, wounds, bleeding gums, piles, sores, bites, and with which to wash the sexual organs of either sex.

In olden days bedridden patients were bathed with diluted Witch-Hazel and laid on a clean sheepskin (Hippocrates mentions it).

The extract is used.

YARROW

Achillea Millefolium. One of my own favourite herbs. It is an excellent herb to put on wounds, and seems to possess remarkable healing properties. It is excellent if you have been out on a winter's night, got wet and cold, and consequently expect a touch of 'flu; a simple Yarrow tea made as soon as possible, and drunk up quickly will make you feel fit and warm.

Drops of the cooled decoction can be squeezed into the ears to relieve many complaints of the ears; rubbed on the head it can strengthen the scalp and hinder the falling out of hair.

Cases have been recorded where epilepsy has been considerably alleviated by a course of Yarrow treatment.

I personally have such great faith in the properties of this herb that I tend to use it particularly in early stages of many diseases and fevers. Certainly it helps many rheumatic patients.

The leaves and the flowers are used.

One or two remedies, such as Lemon and Liquorice are so commonly imported that no difficulty should be experienced in buying them when required.

Please take care to use herbs as directed, and do not exceed the recommended doses.

epilogue

This book gives you a brief outline of the uses of herbs. Mankind still knows comparatively little about the properties of the botanic life on this planet; it is true to say that he would benefit much more by researching the flora of the world rather than the minerals. There is a Brazilian nut whose oil can be used as a substitute for petrol! The extraordinary gloss of Vietnamese lacquer is produced by the use of the Cay Son sap from the *Rhus Vernicifera.* The best known remedy for atomic burns is made from Cleopatra's Aloe!

Mentioning the word atomic reminds me that the real casualties in any atomic war would be the survivors who would have to create civilization from the ruins. Their chief worry would be the supply of medicines and foods—the medicines could only come from herbs! Most forms of radiational fall-out pass quite quickly through plant life and settle in the land beneath them. We must preserve our knowledge of simple, effective and safe herbal medicine—we never know when all Mankind may need it to survive.

Nor is this theory of botanic medicine so neglected as formerly; other branches of medicine are paying tribute to its effectiveness. In 1967 the Royal Society of Medicine received a report confirming that liquorice contains one of the most effective answers to gastric ulcers. In " *Green Medicine* " M. Kreig reports that the much neglected Sarsaparilla actually is now acknowledged as having all the properties formerly attributed to it by the Indians of Central America.

As regards safety remember that the simple herbs

are in their natural form; modern allopathic medicine too often concentrates drugs in a quintessential strength as it were, which is too overpowering for a sick person.

I do recommend readers to cultivate their own herbs even if only in a window-box or in pots, look after them and they will look after you in return.

I conclude this work with two messages, the first is for your enjoyment—leave a sprig of thyme in a bottle of cider an hour before you drink it, I fancy you'll enjoy the added taste. The second is that in writing this book I wish you all health, and I believe that there is no greater possession on Earth than good health.

DONALD LAW

Ph.D., D.B.M., Dip.D., Psy.D.,

F.I.A.L., Dip.I.F.P.C., A.S.T.A.,

etc.

ALLSPICE

(Jamaica Pepper), not be confused with mixed spice. Used in pickles, with grilled meat, in fruit puddings and cakes.

ANGELICA

Mild, pleasant, the crystallized stalks used to decorate cakes and puddings. Finely chopped, added to fruit cakes.

BALM

Fragrant, lemony in taste and scent, used in meat stuffings, soup and stews. Add tiny sprigs to drinks and fruit punches.

BASIL

A herb with a pungent, slightly peppery flavour, to use in soups, stews, sauces. Good with tomato, beans, peas, marrow.

BAY

The dried leaf of a Mediterranean laurel, used in soups, stews, many meat and fish dishes, and in Bouquet Garni.

BORAGE

A herb with a mild pleasant cucumber flavour, added to long summer drinks, wine and fruit cups, especially Pimms.

CAPERS

Principally used to flavour sauces, such as Sauce Tartare, also served with mutton. The smaller the caper buds, the milder.

CARAWAY

The seeds, with a pungent and aromatic flavour, are used in cakes, biscuits and bread, in cheese and with boiled cabbage.

CASSIA

The inner bark of the cinnamon tree, like cinnamon in flavour, but coarser. Cheaper, it is sometimes sold as ground cinnamon.

CAYENNE PEPPER

Very hot and pungent, made from dried pods of small red capsicum. Used very sparingly in curries, savoury rice, cheese straws.

CELERY SEED

Strong in flavour, used to flavour soups and stews. Ground into powder, as celery salt, it is used as a table condiment.

CHERVIL

Improves flavour of other herbs, used in salads, stews, Sauce Bernaise, Bouquet Garni. Has slight flavour of aniseed.

CHILLI

A very hot variety of capsicum, used very sparingly in pickles and hot sauces, and in Chilli Con Carne and other spicy foods.

CHIVES

Fleshy green shoots are cut as required, have a delicate flavour of onion. Used in salads and stuffings, on fish, etc.

CINNAMON

Bark of cinnamon tree, the powder flavours desserts, cakes, biscuits. Stick cinnamon is used in mulled wine, spiced wine, pickles.

CLOVE

Dried shrub flower with strongly aromatic flavour, used sparingly with cooked apple. Infusion flavours cakes, biscuits, sweets.

CORIANDER

The fragrant seeds are used as ingredient of curry spice, also to flavour gin. Leaves, strongly scented, can be added to salads.

DILL

An aromatic herb similar to fennel, but more delicate in flavour. Used in soups, stews, salad dressing and potato salad.

FENNEL

Not to be confused with Italian vegetable of the same name. Use as garnish, or with fish, especially mackerel or salmon.

FENUGREEK

A member of the bean family. The beans, dried and ground, are used in curry powder. Fenugreek is seldom used in any other way.

GARLIC

Has a powerful acrid taste. The 'cloves' of the bulb-like root is used sparingly with meat and other savoury dishes, and salads.

GINGER

A root, used to flavour chutneys, curries, sauces, wines and cordials. Powdered or crystallized it is added to cakes and biscuits.

HORSE-RADISH

A hot astringent root, grated to make a sauce traditionally to serve with roast beef. Also excellent with beetroot salad.

HYSSOP

A member of the mint family. Pungent, aromatic leaves are used in salads and soups. Hyssop honey is highly prized.

continued

BEANS
Basil, Savory

BEETROOT SALAD
Horse-radish

BERNAISE SAUCE
Chervil

BISCUITS
Caraway, Cinnamon, Clove, Nutmeg

BOILED CABBAGE
Caraway

BOILED FOWL
Parsley

BOILING MEAT
Peppercorn

BOUQUET GARNI
Bay, Chervil, Marjoram, Sage, Thyme

BRAWN
Peppercorn

CAKES
Caraway, Cinnamon, Clove, Ginger, Mace, Nutmeg, Poppy Seeds

CHICKEN
Paprika, Tarragon

CHILLI CON CARNE
Chilli

CURRIES
Cayenne Pepper, Ginger, Turmeric

DESSERTS
Nutmeg

EGG DISHES
Sorrel, Thyme

FANCY BREAD
Poppy Seeds

FISH
Bay, Fennel (esp. Mackerel or Salmon), Marjoram, Mustard Sauce (Mackerel), Parsley, Thyme

FRIED FISH
Parsley

FRUIT CAKE
Angelica

FRUIT CUPS
Pennyroyal

FRUIT SALAD
Mint

GAME MARINADE
Juniper

GOOSE
Sage

GRILLED MEAT
Allspice

LAMB
Marjoram, Mint

LAMBS TONGUES
Mustard

continued